CHRIST IN ˹

CW00549038

- Here, John Vincent sets out the developed in the earliest years of BritꞮꞨꞮ ꞮꞮꞮꞮꞮ ꞮꞮꞮꞮ have since become fundamental to the discipline. But that is not all! For John has devoted his life as a committed disciple of the Urban Christ and this radical edge speaks through every page as he describes how he has continued to develop the operation of the discipline for which he laid the foundations. *Rt Rev. Laurie Green, formerly Bishop of Bradwell*

- Few, if any, know the inner city better than John Vincent. His commitment to it for nearly fifty years has given him an unrivalled vantage point from which to interpret the Bible, human society and the Christian gospel. *Christ in the City* sums up his life's work and makes available to readers a unique treasury of personal experience and rich insights. No one concerned with Christian ministry can afford to ignore it. *Canon Prof. John Rogerson, former Head of Biblical Studies, Sheffield*

- John Vincent, as a radical Methodist minister working in the heart of towns and cities in northern England, was making 'waves' in the Church and beyond when I was still at school in the 1960s. For over half a century, he has spoken prophetically to the Church and to the wider world, and here he distils a lifetime's experience of ministry in the inner city in this definitive book. *Rev. Dr. Neil Richardson, New Testament Scholar, former Methodist President*

- John J. Vincent coined the term 'Urban Theology' in 1969 and has remained the central inspiration for honing the concept and for shaping and implementing the practice. Now this key book reflects on more than forty years' experience and distils the wisdom of the corporate venture of the Urban Theology Unit. In the process the reader is invited to progress from thinking about the idea of urban theology to engaging with the practice of urban theologising. *Canon Prof. Leslie J. Francis. Centre for Religions and Education, Warwick*

- For any that find themselves in urban ministry with inadequate theological resources on which to draw, this book will introduce them to new and creative ways of thinking. For those that have toiled longer in the city, it will be a source of great encouragement, especially in the contemporary context of austerity Britain. It is, in the best sense of the word, provocative. *Canon Dr. Alan Billings, former Director of Centre for Ethics and Religion, Lancaster*

FAITH AND PRACTICE

A Series of Theological Practice

1. JOHN W. ROGERSON
   NINE O'CLOCK SERVICE and Other Sermons
2. JOHN J. VINCENT
   CHRIST IN THE CITY

Forthcoming

3. IAN K. DUFFIELD
   WORKING WITH THE GOSPEL IN YOUR PLACE
4. NOEL G. IRWIN
   DIRTY HANDS THEOLOGY: FAITH IN THE TROUBLES

Other Titles to Follow

BRITISH LIBERATION THEOLOGY

Series Editors: Chris Rowland and John Vincent

1. LIBERATION THEOLOGY UK
2. GOSPEL FROM THE CITY
3. LIBERATION SPIRITUALITY
4. BIBLE AND PRACTICE
5. FOR CHURCH AND NATION

Christ in the City is obtainable, price £12.00 p&p £3.00. British Liberation Theology series volumes are available price £7.50, p&p 2.50p. All of the first volumes (1, 2, 3 & 4) can be obtained price £15 plus £5.00 p&p. Normal discounts (35%) are available to booksellers. Quantities of 10 or over are available to other organisations at a special discount (25%). Cheques to Urban Theology Unit.

Details from http://www.utusheffield.org.uk

Christ in the City

The Dynamics of Christ in Urban Theological Practice

JOHN J. VINCENT

Sheffield
Urban Theology Unit

Front Cover: Pitsmoor Study House, 208-210 Abbeyfield Road

Christ in the City

© Copyright, John J. Vincent, 2013
First Published 2013

ISBN: 978-0-907490-13-5

Urban Theology Unit is Registered Charity No: 1115390
Company Limited by Guarantee Reg Number. 5763786

URBAN THEOLOGY UNIT
210 Abbeyfield Road
Sheffield
S4 7AZ

Typeset by Rachel O'Leary at the Urban Theology Unit
Printed by City Print Service, Sheffield

CONTENTS

Chapter Two

THE DYNAMICS
OF CHRIST

Chapter Three

OUTWORKINGS IN
DISCIPLESHIP AND MINISTRY

Chapter Four

OUTWORKINGS IN COMMUNITY AND POLITICS

EPILOGUE

PREFACE

This volume is an invitation to colleagues and readers to join in the adventure of constant new creation which has come to be called Urban Theology—or, as I prefer nowadays to call it, Urban Theologising. It is a longish Part Three of a trilogy, which continues some of the practical ministry stories of *Into the City* (1982), and *Hope from the City* (2000), but especially develops the methods, theory, and theology behind them—and tells other stories from other ministries and the national scene.

The invitation is intended to involve three groups of readers. First of all, I want to bring Christian disciples and workers into a process of discovery that will hopefully develop what they are already into, and show them how they are already "doing theology", and also how they can develop their discipleship by looking at different ways in which Gospel stories and insights might open up significant new avenues for practice and reflection. I hope that some of these stories and insights will make disciples in every place say, "Well, if they can do things like this where they are, what could we do where we are?" The methodologies employed work in very different contexts, as people found in the widely used *Journey* programme (2003), a course which popularises some of the methods here.

Second, I want to assist colleagues in theological circles. My own efforts in the area of theology have always started in the discipline of New Testament Studies, and particularly studies of the Gospels. But my choice—or my calling—has been to be a theologian of Discipleship, which necessarily puts action before reflection. My ministry has been in the location of the urban because this seemed to me to be the obvious place in our time for a would-be disciple of Jesus to be. This Gospel call ended me up in what developed as Contextual Theology—doing theology within the limitations and opportunities of a particular context, in my case the urban. So I worked in housing estate Wythenshawe, town centre Rochdale, and then from 1970 inner city Sheffield.

In the last decade, I have been involved in the British New Testament Society and its Seminar on Use and Influence, in which the concept of Practice Interpretation has been helped along, until the stage now where a whole series of Practice Interpretation volumes is appearing. Theology from the City, as I have discovered it, is a striking *reprise* of some things I first learned from the Gospels, especially Mark. I hope that others will be drawn into similar discoveries.

Third, I want to celebrate with fellow practitioners in Urban Theology, and hopefully to push along some current projects and open up some new possibilities. I have leaned heavily in places upon the work of some of my colleagues in UTU—fellow teachers, students, community workers, urban disciples. Beside this, I have drawn upon the experience of Ashram Community and its inner city projects. Connections with urban practitioners elsewhere have also been important, not least since 1999 through the Urban Theology Collective at St. Deiniol's Library. National networks like the triennial Urban Congress and international consultations on Urban Mission have likewise been fruitful and expanding occasions. This *Christ in the City* is in fact launched at the September 2013 Jesus in the City Congress in Manchester.

I hope that others will be drawn into this very ecumenical urban mission family, not least now that Fresh Expressions calls for innovative incarnational urban projects. It has often been observed that the stories of Sheffield Inner City Ecumenical Mission told in *Into the City* and *Hope from the City* look like Fresh Expressions before their time. Those stories are not repeated here, though some of their theological fruits are pressed, alongside many more, in this attempt to work out some significant elements for present and future Urban Theology—which is essentially and dialogically Urban Missioning and Gospel Theologising done by turns, as I hope to show.

I feel that I owe an apology to readers that this book has been so long in appearing. Since I first coined the term "Urban Theology" in 1969, I have lived with it as it grew, developing also Contextual Theology, Liberation Theology, Outworkings, Theological Practice, Practice Interpretation, and Endogenous Theology, as labels for our experiences. I wanted to get some perspectives on all this—backwards, sideways, and hopefully forwards. So the formulations here describe where this "Urban Gospel Theology Creation" has landed at present. I have to admit that the lack of a definitive piece on Urban Theology from myself has meant that others have used the term but in the process somewhat changed its contents.

Here, now, at last, all is revealed, such as it is, with some attempt to plot the way thus far, though UTU's history as such still needs to be written—a task to which we are addressing ourselves.

My debts to others are numerous, and I record my cordial thanks to them all. Former doctoral students, now authorities in the field, Christine Dodd, Laurie Green, Ian Duffield, Alan Billings, Andrew Davey and Joe Aldred, are my fellow-travellers. Contemporaries over the decades have given freely of their time to come and teach with us—Pauline Webb, John D. Davies, Austin Smith, Ian Fraser, Laurie Green, Chris Rowland, Margaret Walsh, and David McLellan. Recent writers in the field will see our ongoing debates continued—Kenneth Leech, Elaine Graham, James Jones, John Atherton, Christopher Baker, Stephen Lowe, Stuart Jordan and Chris Shannahan. I am especially indebted to co-workers in New Testament Gospel Studies sharing in the development of Practice Interpretation— Philip Davies, Leslie Francis, Timothy Gorringe, Christine Jones, Louise Laurence, John Riches, John Rogerson, Christopher Rowland, Ian Wallis, and Gerald West. Colleagues at UTU have heard much of it before— Christine Jones, Debbie Herring, Ian Duffield, Robin Pagan, and Noel Irwin. Recent students and friends are fellow-provocateurs—plus ten current doctoral students completing their work. Institutionally and personally, we at UTU owe much to our old university collaborators at New York Theological Seminary with the Doctor of Ministry Programme—Bill Webber, Richard Snyder, and Norman Gottwald, and also at Sheffield University with the first MPhil/PhD programme in Contextual, Urban and Liberation Theologies –especially Loveday Alexander, David Clines, Diane Edelmann, Cheryl Exum, John Rogerson, and Keith Whitelam. Similarly we thank our more recent university collaborators with the MPhil/PhD Programme—Martin Stringer and colleagues at Birmingham University, and with the MA Programme— Andrew Village and colleagues at York St John University. At present we are commencing a new relationship with Manchester University through our new membership of the Luther King House Consortium. Finally, I record my thanks for the computer gifts and personal support of Judith Simms and Rachel O'Leary in the UTU office. Author's proceeds go as usual to UTU, as they continue to hold my writing work as part of their mission. Thanks, again, to them. UTU thus take over Volume 3 in the now demised Epworth Press trilogy started with *Into the City* and *Hope from the City*.

PROLOGUE

There is, of course, only a *relative* difference between the church, human and community issues in the *inner* city and those elsewhere in the contemporary world. Dwellers in Hathersage and Heanor are also human beings. Administrators and executives in the city centre (who are also Hathersage and Heanor dwellers!) are also urban human beings; suburban church worshippers are also urban human beings.

But both are, by world standards, only a tiny percentage of people. They have, by comparison, already far more than their share of intelligent, committed Christians. They have the money, the education, the background and the friends which make them able to "cope". By placing their theological resources so far also in these contexts, the churches have merely brought further sophistication to the sophisticated. By placing theological students, ministers, and lay people alongside the already affluent, the "message" of theology itself has already to some extent been predetermined. A limited vantage point is secured, in which middle-class presuppositions, assumptions, standards, expectations, experiences, hopes, life-styles, and relationships can be assumed, which coalesces more or less completely with the attitudes of the academic world or of suburbia. Here the churches' intellectual and missional work has until now normally been done.

By placing our Unit in the inner city, a different vantage-point is secured. Different presuppositions, assumptions, standards, expectations, experiences, hopes, life-styles and relationships can be entered into. A context is created in which the academic and missional tasks of the Church look vastly different from what they seemed in the context of university or suburbia, where most church colleges have been thus far placed.

The medium is not the message. But the situation determines both the kind of questions it is assumed the gospel exists to answer, and the kind of answers which our Christian culture assumes we ought to be giving. We do not yet know everything about how to do it differently. But we are convinced that the attempt to find out is enormously important.

John J. Vincent, "Innovation in Great Britain—
the Sheffield Urban Theology Unit", *Learning in Context,* 1973: 128.

TO
IAN K DUFFIELD
and
NOEL G. IRWIN,
Colleagues and Friends
and Co-Labourers

Chapter One

URBAN

THEOLOGISING

1. *A TALE OF TWO CITIES*

In November 2009, a Sheffield University Geography Department research team published a report, *A Tale of Two Cities: The Sheffield Project*. It recorded striking contemporary facts about Sheffield as a "divided city", which we in Sheffield's north east inner city Burngreave/Pitsmoor still experience:

- Burngreave residents live 7–13.5 years less than those living on the other side of Sheffield. Men in Burngreave only live to 74 and women to 77, whilst those in Hallam live to 81 and 89.
- From 1971 to 2001, higher educated people rose in Brightside from 1.3% to 7.7%, but in Hallam from 11.3% to 37.5%.
- 2% in Ecclesall live in properties in Council Band A, 99.3% in Shiregreen.
- In 2005–2007, Brightside had 716 Road Traffic casualties; Hallam had only 294.
- Babies in Abbeyfield are 5 times as likely to be of critical low birth weight, compared to Ranmoor. Children under 5 are far more likely to have damaged teeth in Abbeyfield and Woodside.
- 75% of young people from Burngreave get their first choice of secondary school, against 95% elsewhere.
- Standardised Mortality Rates in Central and Brightside constituencies are a third above the national average and twice as high as Hallam constituency.

Our MP, David Blunkett, points out in the *Sheffield Telegraph* that the whole of Sheffield misses out from government funding, because the very affluent west brings the average wealth up. The problem is not the poor in the east, but the rich in the west! My conclusion was that I started a new campaign—not "Make Poverty History" but "Make Affluence History". Blunkett continues:

> In simple terms, to narrow the gap between rich and poor, between inequalities in education and health, asset wealth and personal income—the family, the neighbourhood and community together have to be targeted. (5 November 2009)

This book comes from the east of Sheffield. Forty years ago, in 1970, we started Pitsmoor Action Group, with joint chairs—Councillor David Blunkett for Labour, Councillor Francis Butler for Liberals, and David Chapman for Conservatives, and myself and Mike Newton as organisers. Recalling this in the following week's *Sheffield Telegraph*, former Councillor Howard Knight writes:

> Some 40 years ago—the start of the period covered by the study—John Vincent (Reverend Dr and Minister of the Sheffield Inner-City Ecumenical Mission) was accurately describing how those who succeeded through education left the inner-city, the professionals (teachers, doctors, police officers, etc) who served the inner city didn't live there, and that the churches were also abandoning the poorest areas. It led him—and others—to initiate a number of projects, including a call to young professionals to reverse the trend. That's how I came to live in—and have never left—Burngreave; a decision I've never regretted (12 November 2009).

The City Council's Fairness Commission Report, *Making Sheffield Fairer* (2012) makes similar points, though concentrates on health issues. The question is still, as I said in a letter to the *Sheffield Telegraph* (14 February 2012), "Who in the Council have the time and money to make sure these and other good ideas get done?"

An article on "Sheffield—Divided City" by myself was in *The Star* for 4 July 1979 (Vincent, 1982: 6-8). Now, as we look ahead, we seek to gather some learnings from these forty years, and to develop some new perspectives.

Wider surveys show that Sheffield is not the only "divided city" in Britain. Indeed, in 2013, recession enforces those divisions. So, hopefully, our stories and our theologies will be parables for the nation. But the basics of our contexts look remarkably similar over the years.

2. THE SHEFFIELD EXPERIENCE

The Sheffield experience for many visitors is that you arrive at the rail station, and walk straight up into the city centre, or take a taxi to the west side where the Sheffield University is. Sheffield is a divided city, and has been so for two centuries. Indeed, if you had arrived at various times in the last forty years, and asked to be taken to Pitsmoor or Burngreave on the east side, the taxi driver might well have said that he didn't go up there, as it was not safe. In 2013, many taxi-drivers are Pakistanis who live here, so they will welcome your journey! Finally, the inner ring road in 2008 has been extended to take traffic around the east of the centre. But it is now even more difficult to find a route that will take you up Spital Hill and into Burngreave Road, or up Rock Street into Pitsmoor. The east is now more cut off from the west than ever. The floods in June 2007 overflowed the Don Valley, and west to east was impassable.

The history is that the first steel works in the 1830s to 1850s opened up the whole of the River Don Valley going eastward to Rotherham, and 90,000 men sweated in the steelworks to produce tanks used on both sides in the First World War, with sulphur fumes totally obliterating the Attercliffe valley from view, and leading to the premature death of millions. When the steel works downsized in the 1970s, some 30,000 men became unemployed, mainly living in the vast housing estates on the north and east of the city—Parson Cross and Shiregreen to the north, Manor to the south. Only in 2000 was my piece of the eastern inner city officially discovered as an area of acute deprivation, and a £52 million ten-year project of New Deal for Communities brought outside experts and resources to the beleaguered area, and co-opted a few locals, myself included, onto the Partnership Board, securing several flagship building redevelopments. The effort to raise standards in law and order, education, housing, health and employment has had some success, but we now receive hundreds of new immigrants each year, not least 500 asylum seekers huddled in overcrowded houses, and this naturally affects all these areas. "Law and Order" have improved, but for eight years we annually have had gun-related fatalities.

Sheffield mythology states it plainly. You make your money in the east, but make your home in the west. Contemporary planning and building still follow the nineteenth century adage. In Burngreave, the city's 2006 Housing Initiative Masterplan squeezed in a few acres of up-market housing near to the Riverside apartments, but reserved a block of "social housing" for the bottom of Ellesmere Road, just up from Spital Hill. The educational divide, despite some significant improvements after "special measures" in one secondary school, continues in a yearly battle for many parents to get their 11 year olds into a secondary school on the west of the city.

In the west end's Weston Park you will find the statue of one of our local heroes, Ebenezer Elliot (1781–1849), who epitomises the cry of the inner city, now as then, against the hegemony of powers arraigned against the common people or the poor. It was a blast, in fact, against the National Anthem, with its redundant plea of "God save the King". It was a cry to God to save the people:

When wilt thou save the people
O God of mercy, when?
The people, Lord, the people,
Not thrones and crowns, but men!
Flowers of Thy heart, O God, are they;
Let them not pass like weeds away,
Their heritage a sunless day.
God save the people!

The "woundedness" of an inner city area (Schneider & Susser, 2003) is a many-sided experience. All the ills of the city are inflicted on the inner city. Drugs, prostitution, crime, homelessness, poverty and decay lead to a feeling of dehumanisation, exclusion and isolation. In the press and media, we are always being "got at". When we go elsewhere in the city—as our children must do to get a better school—we are "stigmatised". We bear in our bodies the marks of our earthly citizenship—yet without the summer riots of 2011 which occurred in some other cities.

3. THE ORIGINS OF URBAN THEOLOGY

Could Theology be any use?

The Term "Urban Theology" was first used by myself at the Inauguration of the Urban Theology Unit in August 1969. The first Prospectus of UTU described its aims in four ways.

1. *Theological Study.* Investigation in depth of the Christian inheritance, in the belief that Christianity represents and indicates a dynamic for healing and change in history and society. The Unit thus provides opportunity for the *study* of theology against the environment of contemporary secular society.

2. *Intern Training.* Exposure to the issues of today through personal involvement in and reflection upon the strategic points in human life in western industrial society. The Unit thus provides for the *training* of laity and clergy in relevant styles of theology, reflection and vocation.

3. *Community Dynamics.* Experimentation with techniques for social change in specific situations, through long term commitment in or involvement with agencies and projects in those situations. The Unit thus provides opportunity for the *engagement* of persons of all ages, not least students and clergy, in community action internships.

4. *Cultural Encounter.* Orientation of thinking and action around the language, culture and customs of post-Christian Britain. The Unit thus provides a practical and theoretical *workshop* for urban, contemporary, cultural, and community studies and experiments.

The Urban Theology Unit was formed as a voluntary society in August 1969, following meetings in Rochdale of theologians and sociologists to set up an Institute of Church and Society in the North-West of Britain. The Unit was intended from the outset to be a community of committed Christians, concerned to bring theology and sociology together to serve the Church and the City. We became a Registered Charity in 1970.

"Urban" was stated as a new *context* for "Theology". One of five "Priorities for the 70s" was described as "Theological Work", which meant that the Unit's main contribution is its concern to wrestle with contemporary theological problems in the light of the challenge and opportunity of the life of modern secular, urban humanity. "This means both a radically contemporary reassessment of the Christian core of faith, and also a radically open examination of the total life of humanity today" (*The Urban Theology Unit*, 1971: 4).

Various Mission Statements have been produced. In 1994, UTU committed itself to:

- the radical Gospel of the Kingdom
- the search for Christian discipleship and vocation in the city
- the empowerment of the poor and the powerless
- the theological and ministerial potential of each Christian
- the specific context in which theology, ministry and action take place
- the participation of people in their own education and liberation

All of this adds up to two obvious conclusions. First, that the phrase "Urban Theology" arose for the first time in the context of UTU in Sheffield, where it functioned variously to describe "A Unit" which was placed in the Urban in order to do Theology there, so that "Urban" went with both Theology as mission and Unit as method. The second conclusion is that there was not originally any "Urban Theology", but rather setting up processes, locations and personnel who would experiment by Doing Theology in the Urban, that is, by "Urban Theologising".

This meant that we had an equal commitment to urban realities, and to theology. We created bases where both could be served—an Inner City Study House and an Alternative Theological Base.

4. AN INNER CITY STUDY HOUSE

In September 1972, we set up UTU in 2 rooms in 233 Abbeyfield Road. Then we put out an appeal to open a Study House, and bought 210 Abbeyfield Road with £3,000 from Sheffield City Council, a £3,000 loan (later gifted) from the Society of the Sacred Mission, and £1,000 from friends. In December 1973 we used the 20 people on the Christmas World

Church Consultation Week to carry our furniture up the road from 233 to 210, which we called Pitsmoor Study House.

The objects of the Pitsmoor Study House were stated as:

- *a place* where new hope for new community can be strengthened in the inner city.
- *a commitment* of people with expertise and humanity who come and live and work in the community, making their talents, skills and resources available to all who need them.
- *a listening-post,* where people can tell their stories, and we can start building up a sense of significance again within communities of tension and need.
- *a research centre,* in the midst of some problems, where men and women of all ages can have time and space to think, find out, and write.

In pursuit of these aims, the House would operate as (a) a house where local community groups can come and "do their thing" in a homely atmosphere; (b) an adult education centre where discussion groups, self-programming classes, and other experimental work in community adult education take place; (c) a resource centre and library, reading room, and work room, where anyone who wishes can come and read and study; and (d) a residential centre, where long and short term adult students from Britain and many parts of the world come and live, involving themselves in the total work of the House and the life of the local community.

Local neighbourhood agendas were our concern from the beginning.

We helped form the Pitsmoor Action Group in 1970. Sheffield Planning Department were busy reconfiguring the area, including possible plans to demolish almost the whole of Burngreave and Pitsmoor. Our first Sheffield Ashram Community House in Andover Street was at the heart of the threatened area. We produced an alternative report in September 1972—*Pitsmoor for Tomorrow.* We succeeded! The threatened housing is nearly all still there today, and the threatened road schemes were abandoned.

Our first courses provided focus for locals and incomers to work at relevant issues. In 1974–75, we had weekly evening courses on Experiments in Education, Welfare Rights, and Community Studies. We held week-long Consultations on Alternative Planning, and The Future of South Yorkshire, and study weeks on Contemporary Thought and on Community, Sociology and Planning. Those who wanted them, plus the Postgraduate/Study Year, had seminars on Mark's Gospel and Luke-Acts (Alan T. Dale), Christian Community and Contemporary Catholic Theology (Austin Smith), Galatians and Mark's Gospel (John D. Davies), and on Feminist Theology (Pauline Webb), Creative Theology, Global Urban Mission, Urban Ministry and Experimental Systematics (led by the part-time staff, Edward S. Kessler, Roy B. Crowder and myself).

5. AN ALTERNATIVE THEOLOGICAL BASE

Models for this were hard to find, and we simply made it up as we went along.

I had studied at Chicago Urban Training Center in 1967 and taught at Boston University School of Theology and New York Theological Seminary in 1969–70. At the latter, George W. Webber was busy creating an alternative theological seminary. The scene is well set by Laurie Green's recent historical record (in Rowland & Vincent, eds, 2013: 34-45). In all this, the works of Ivan Illich and Paulo Freire were vital elements. Immediately on my arrival in Sheffield in September 1970 I became engaged at several points in World Council of Churches projects. There were periodic consultations with others in Britain concerned with theological education and with training for urban mission (Green, 2003: 34-37). During 1972–74 we had consultations on "Church Leaders: Towards a Policy", "Theology and Church in the Inner City", and "The Contemporary Search for Ministry", "Theology and Church in the Contemporary City", "Theological Education in the Modern City". Then, we hosted "Alternative Theological Education" in 1979, a major consultation which issued in a booklet of this title (Vincent, ed., 1979). Many other conference reports were published in the *New City* journal series.

In an article in a WCC publication, *Learning in Context* (1973), I described our efforts as novel in four ways, connected with location, public, medium and freedom, as follows.

1. *Location.* We are in the modern secular city, but especially the inner city, "where the issues of technology, economics, and so on, are addressed from a context which itself is acutely at risk in such matters, and in which the *dramatis personae* are the people undergoing change in an acute form, and the people who live and work with them" (126). The Unit is located among the people, where we function from two old houses. "As students live in two local community houses, or in flats or "digs" in the area, they learn *how* to learn in a human way."

2. *Public.* I wrote, "We may ask, what is the *public* that theology has in view?" By placing theology within the university setting, the answer is presumably "mainly fellow academics". By setting itself among the people in the inner city, Urban Theology Unit makes it easier for other publics to be identified and addressed (127).

Four publics were identified.

First, there were "*the Christian individuals and Christian communities* at the grassroots, whether they be in large cathedral or central hall, small working-class gospel mission, suburban congregation, or whatever." "Seldom do they speak. We try to encourage them to speak".

A second public was "our more immediate *neighbours in the inner city.*"

Often, they are the underprivileged, the disadvantaged, the deprived. Often, they include immigrants, nomads, vagrants, unmarried mothers, flat-dwellers, drop-outs, unemployed teenagers. Frequently, they are those at the "bottom" of society, who face the complex issues and challenges of contemporary urban life with least preparedness. Here, we are concerned not merely with those who live at the "grass roots" of society, but at the "withered roots", as we sometimes describe our "patch" in Pitsmoor (127).

Thirdly, there were the people *alongside and outside the faith*, who have long ago disassociated themselves from the scene represented by the little local church-based groups, but are still people for whom, faith declares, the Christian mysteries operate, and who can get involved in gospel action even when they do not name the name.

Fourthly, there were *the bureaucrats and experts* who look over our shoulders—the politicians, the planners, the architects, the sociologists, the social workers, the councillors, the civil servants, the community development officers, the welfare agencies, the suburban intellectuals, the church "leaders". Often, they ask us questions.

I'm not sure that the new "Public Theology" in 2013 recognises the controlling power of *different* publics!

3. *Medium.* The location of inner city was also felt to constitute the *medium.* A new vantage point was secured. As the Prologue to the present book repeats:

> A context is created in which the academic and missional tasks of the Church look vastly different from what they seemed in the context of university or suburbia, where most church colleges have been thus far placed. The medium is not the message, but the situation determines both the kind of questions it is assumed the gospel exists to answer, and the kind of answers which our Christian culture assumes we ought to be giving. We do not yet know everything about how to do it differently. But we are convinced that the attempt to find out is enormously important (128).

4. *Freedom.* Our independence from denominational or academic control undoubtedly imposes restrictions, but we had "freedom to try to be authentic to the Gospel in a place where the Gospel has not always been heard" (129).

These four elements have continued throughout our years in varied ways, but still with the same basic characteristics and differentiations. In 2013, UTU opens a "Teaching Suite" in the City Centre at the Victoria Hall Methodist Church Victoria Hall. We take on now also aspects of a new Location, Public, Medium, and Freedom, and discover what from 1973 is still relevant.

6. ALTERNATIVE PLANNING

In April 1974, the Metropolitan County Council of South Yorkshire was born. UTU worked, with a group of planners, on the South Yorkshire Structure Plan, which declared:

It is concerned with general issues underlying planning, with the quality of life, with the values in a society, with what people think is important in the future of South Yorkshire.

Great, we said. So we formed a Consultative Group, with locals and planners, plus Bryan Coates and Roy Darke from Sheffield University. Our report, *South Yorkshire in Search of a Soul* in 1975, had chapters from both, plus Jenny Carpenter (a Planning Consultant), Ed Kessler (a planner and theologian, on UTU staff), and myself from UTU.

My chapters were on "Alternative Planning" and "An Alternative South Yorkshire". They were written after some hundreds of hours with planners, councillors, and local groups. We had, as usual for Planners, an excellent team from the Authority. However, my chapter on "Alternative Planning" (22-25) stated:

"Planning is not evil: it is Tragic." I said it to comfort one of our local planners after a particularly gruelling evening at the Study House. I think it is true. Many of the things which planners want to do are wholly right and good. But this book shows yet again that we do not know how to do them. The methods and presuppositions of contemporary planning often effectively prevent the right thing being done, or good resulting. We need new presuppositions, a new orientation (22).

I named four essentials for Alternative Planning.

1. *A Satisfaction Orientation.* Don't begin with "What's wrong? We'll fix it." Begin with "What's right? We'll build on it." So: begin with peoples' stories. Maximise what is already there. Set up Planners at the neighbourhood level. Begin with life as it is, and improve it. Use "satisfaction" as a visible criterion for policies.

2. *Community and County Democracy.* Develop a complementary power-base "at the bottom". "Participation" must be on the peoples' terms, not on the Planners'. Power must be de-sectionalised (from special interest committees and "pots" of money).

3. *Get to Real Issues.* Deal with stubborn factors unlikely to change, with growing imbalances between groups, with the problem that the "voice" of Sheffield comes from its south-west, with the peculiar situation of South Yorkshire regionally and nationally.

4. *Four Options for the Future.* I concluded with four possible ways to go:

(1.) Leave things alone, alleviating where possible the worst conditions in "bad" areas, and seeking to attract more "good" ones. This would merely mean steady deterioration, and probably a diminishment of "good" areas also. These would not be acceptable.

(2.) Balance up the "bad" areas in the county by discrimination against the few "good" areas, housing, shopping and industries. This would merely drive away the few "good" areas. This would not be acceptable.

(3.) Introduce vast economic, social and amenity improvement and rehabilitation of the "bad" areas, housing, shopping and industries. This is, by and large, the intention behind present planning policies. But who will determine what is brought in?

(4.) Affirm South Yorkshire as an "alternative" style county, financing grass-roots improvement in the "bad" areas, housing, shopping and industries. This is the option argued for here (24).

I elaborated the latter in a chapter on "Alternative County" (26-27), in which I argued for a different set of policies: Maximise the mini-scale, cash in on our history (of Little Mesters, Co-ops, Anti-Establishmentism, Closed Shops), heed the signs of the times (people taking up allotments, doing DIY, working at home, moving back into inner cities), and investigate some alternatives. But, of course, the Council went for No. 3, with the hope that that would trickle down into No. 2. No. 4 remained undone.

Later, in the present book, planning issues recur constantly. I am not sure that we have moved very much forward since these early experiences.

7. ALTERNATIVE THEOLOGICAL EDUCATION

The purpose behind all this was both missional and strategic—to rescue theology from its suburban, ecclesiastical, and academic captivities, and to restore it to Christianity as the "second step" behind Christian discipleship practice and experience. So I set out (in Vincent, ed., 1977: 6-8) seven aspects of an "Alternative Theological Education", which ran as follows:

1. For Academics, Discipleship. For Professors with students, we have leaders with disciples. We are perhaps one of the "theological action-stations built around a charismatic Socrates" envisaged by W.A. Visser't Hooft.

2. For Denomination, World. For Denominational seminaries, partisan, partial and church-centred, we open community houses, alongside local people, biased to the poor, centred on issues. Theology in the 1960s said: "the World is the agenda". We now add "Theology is what we bring to it".

3. For Professions, Vocations. The Professional Minister or Theologian with trainees is replaced by People Called, who teach from their situation-sensitive practice. The committed vocational disciple is the key interpreter.

4. For Hierarchy, Community. For Superior with novices, we substitute "a Community, with people judging and supporting each other", with Theology as "Do-It-Yourself adventures, in which all are learners".

5. For Status, Simplicity. Usually, "Theology is taken over to provide a rationale and justification for the lifestyle and interests of middle-class suburban people". This is replaced by "Jesus the friend of publicans and sinners", in "the only theological institution in Britain with outside toilets", plus "long-term commitment with short-term financing".

The people in the next room or the next house are often the dropouts (or the committed drop-ins), the outcasts, the welfare recipients, people outside the churches, people experimenting with survival. Inevitably, we begin to learn a new theology from the New Testament—which deals with such people and situations (7).

6. For Priestly, Franciscan. "For the Priest being paid to do his piece in the temple, Jesus substitutes the apostle being given a bed for the night". Francis-like Jesus followers become "acted parables", and set up places for their life.

7. For Rationalism, Faith. For theology as "faith seeking understanding" we substitute "faith seeking action". Theology as "the Christian story and what Christians have done with it" means we work at "commitment, passion, group-loyalty, relationships and 'call'".

8. RADICAL, URBAN, CONTEXTUAL

In 1973, 1974 and 1975, we held Easter Conferences on "Contemporary Theology". Out of them developed the essays, *Stirrings* (Vincent, ed., 1976). The central argument of the essays is that we were developing a post-*Honest to God* "Christ-centred Radicalism". It was Christ-centred as being a theology based on the Jesus story. It was Radical as "thoroughgoing, basic, practical, secular, distinctive, extreme" (105-106). It was an Action-Theology as being based on discipleship and activity based on the Jesus story. It was a view of faith as Action-Commitment. God was the "Predicate" of all this, Politics its objective manifestation, Liturgy its place of Rehearsal, and Making Disciples its practical outcome (107-122).

Apart from our own work in UTU in earlier biblical work as in Conferences on "Search for Gospel" (1973), the colleagues elsewhere doing similar things were the *Theology in Action* groups of East Asia, and other World Council of Churches urban/rural projects (Vincent, ed., 1976: 121-122).

Some of these colleagues also used terms like Black Theology, Feminist Theology, Latin-American Theology. In that context, we began to develop the concept of an Urban Theology. All of these came to be summarised under the heading of Liberation Theologies.

Each of these theologies is also part of the wider family of Contextual Theologies. In Apartheid South Africa, the work of Liberation Theology which led to the Kairos Document of 1985 had to be carried on under the heading of Contextual Theology. But the term itself has gained recognition over the last two decades.

When in 1991 Professor John Rogerson invited me to be a spare-time Honorary Lecturer in the Biblical Studies Department of Sheffield University, and asked if I would supervise some doctoral students, he asked, "What in?" Immediately, from some subconscious formulation, I replied, "Contextual, Urban and Liberation Theologies." So was born the environment which has pioneered development in the area of Contextual Theologies.

Three Contextual Theologians give us different aspects of Theology as Contextual.

Robert Schreiter (1985: 20-21) argues that a Contextual Theology is derived from three basic elements—the Good News of Jesus Christ, its being incarnate in "the reality of those who bring it to us" who are "enmeshed in situations and communities", and also "the culture within which the incarnation occurs", with all its values, symbols, meanings, hopes and dreams.

Working also in an inner city context, Kenneth Leech says:

When I use the term 'contextual theology' I refer to theology which is consciously pursued in relation to specific communities or to specific issues in the world; which seeks constantly to understand, and relate to, these communities or issues; and which seeks both to bring to bear the resources of theological tradition upon them, and to learn from them in a way which enriches theology and perhaps calls much of it into question (Leech, 2006a: 155).

Laurie Green concludes that Contextual Theology means we "rejoice to find ourselves among kindred spirits"—black theology, feminist theology, rural theology, urban theology—"a many-voiced theology" (Green, 2003: 164). Each one has the same four elements—listening to the local stories, analysing the information, theological reflection, and active responses (165-170).

The nature and method of Contextual Theology, to me, is as follows:

First, each Contextual Theology has to begin with a new analysis, a new 'view from below', a new 'Situation Analysis'. This 'view from below' is primarily that of all the people, or at least some typical people, who belong to the Context. From them and from this standpoint, the process continues in subjecting all the experiences, people, alliances, structures, systems, powers, victims, operators, operations and results of the Context to in-depth study, critique and evaluation.

Second, alongside and into that process is fed also a similarly analytical and critical reading and discernment of some part or parts of the biblical and theological traditions. They also came out of contexts, and the modes of analysis, discernment and conceptual development visible in them might well assist our understanding of our contexts (Riches, 2010).

Third, the two bodies of material are brought into dynamic interplay. The present socio-cultural analysis of the context, and the revisited socio-cultural analyses of pieces of scripture and theology, are brought into dialogue. Out of this dynamic interplay will come relevant practice, projects, discipleship and spirituality. Then, out of them, will come the new creation, the new context's own new Contextual Theology (Duffield, Jones & Vincent, 2000: 26).

9. AS LIBERATION THEOLOGY

I have often said that in UTU we were following a Gospel-based methodology, based on a Contextual Bible practice, and then discovered that others elsewhere were doing similarly, and calling it Liberation Theology. In 1996 I declared:

I'm happy to use the term "liberation theology" because people will talk about it. I've been talking about a gospel theology and an urban theology for twenty five years, and no-one takes any notice at all (Jones, 1996: 88).

As Laurie Green's article, "Liberation Theology and Urban Theology" (Rowland & Vincent, eds, 2013: 34-43) makes clear, we followed a Gospel-style practice, and moved into action on the basis of it, and called it "Urban Theology". Later, we discovered that people elsewhere in the world were using the Gospel as a spur to action in their contexts—and were calling it Liberation Theology. So, suddenly, the Urban Theology had become a Liberation Theology. Well, yes, it did belong to the same family of liberation theologies—Urban stood beside Feminist, Black, South American and other liberation theologies. But I still regretted that "we are jealous of others' theologies but will not forge our own" (Vincent, 1981: 13).

So, I attempted to write "a liberation style biblical theology on the basis of my own experience in inner city Sheffield" in *Into the City* (Vincent, 1982: 14-17). Then, I argued that John Wesley similarly did a contextual theology alongside the poor, "Theology from the Bottom"—which made us both liberation theologians (Vincent, 1984: 69).

In July 1988, Chris Rowland and I called together a group of likely colleagues who agreed to set up a British Liberation Theology Consultation and Celebration Weekend, the first of which was held in Upholland College, near Wigan, in 1989, with subsequent gatherings in Wistaston Hall, near Crewe (Mike Simpson in Rowland & Vincent, eds., 1999: 74-79). These continued bi-annually until 2005, with colleagues like Margaret Walsh, Ian Fraser, Laurie Green, Austin Smith, Margaret Hebblethwaite, Frank Regan, David Rhodes, Bridget Rees, and Simon Barrow.

Partly connected with this, Chris Rowland and I edited a series of four volumes under the general title *British Liberation Theology*. In the first volume, I found myself commenting:

Very few have the good fortune which I enjoy, of being alongside the poor, of being involved in practical community and mission work in deprived areas and poor churches, on the one hand, and also being involved in study and teaching in practical theology, on the other. I must admit that the two places in which I work – the Sheffield Inner City Ecumenical Mission (SICEM) as the community and mission commitment, and the Urban Theology

Unit as the study and teaching commitment – were more or less my own creation, designed precisely to secure what to me had always been the essential mix, if one was to be Christian, let alone a theologian. Together they provide the essential co-existence and mutual play of deep, long-term engagement within a piece of "the world", and prolonged theological reflection and work there. Such, at any rate, has been my life since 1970. It is a peculiar accident of fortune that exactly that mix turns out to be the way that liberation theology has to be done (Rowland & Vincent, eds., 1995: 29).

All liberation theology is contextual, so my theology is a liberation theology based on my context. As my context is that popularised as "urban priority area", it is the context of upwards of 15 million out of Britain's 65 million population. So that it is not a specialist or restricted context, such as a university or a suburban context might be. But it is, nevertheless, also a special context.

So: I seek to be a disciple in the inner city, and theologise on the basis of it. The nearest model in our time to this project-centred theology-practice of Jesus and Jesus communities in the historic times of Jesus and the early Church is to be found in Liberation Theology. I had found that our practice in the Inner City based on the Gospels and on Jesus led us into the activity known elsewhere as Liberation Theology (Vincent, 1981: 13-18).

Later, I realised that our emphasis on Project, again, reflects the burden and the practice of Liberation Theology. Ivan Petrella has sought to recall Liberation Theology precisely to this emphasis on Project. He calls for what he describes as "institutional imagination":

Institutional imagination requires that liberation theology cease to think in terms of monolithic wholes and recognize the contingent nature of institutions. Instead of seeing a world made up of large building blocks offering two (or a few) options, the world should be seen as constructed from myriad tiny blocks that can be mixed, shifted and reconstituted for creating the world liberation theologians seek (Petrella, 2006: 111).

Crucially, he goes on, this can "envision step by step historical projects far beyond the mere denunciation of capitalism". Capitulation to an unchangeable capitalism as "a monolithic and practically inescapable social reality" is thus avoided. Likewise, theology's disappearance into "hope" for some eschatological or millenarian conclusion is also avoided.

Petrella in fact insists that the theologian contributes to Projects as much as the grassroots:

It was a mistake to think that historical projects can emerge only from the grassroots and that the theologian must wait until they so emerge. This assumes that there is a divide between the theologian and the community with which he or she identifies; the theologian reads theologically a historical project that emerges first from the community. Instead, this divide must be rejected and overcome. The theologian must be seen as an integral part of the community and thus through his or her work may contribute to the possible emergence of historical projects within a neighbourhood, a region, a nation, and even the globe (Petrella, 2006: 148).

This practice of community practitioners as theologians is precisely the one which all UTU efforts have been concerned to support and develop.

My own experience of four decades can thus echo what Petrella has written:

Liberation theology must be wrested from the stranglehold of church and academy. Both church and academy domesticate it by constraining liberation theology within a limited and 'proper' definition of theology. Only by releasing itself from this stranglehold can liberation theology's necessarily interdisciplinary nature come forth (Petrella, 2006: 149).

Many issues arise connected with Liberation Theology's importance for our future work in Britain in the coming decade. Our recent essays volume, *For Church and Nation* (Rowland & Vincent, eds., 2013) details many of them. They should be consulted at this point, and are not repeated here.

10. URBAN LIBERATION THEOLOGY

The emphasis upon specific Projects as the aim and manifestation of Liberation Theology brings me back to the origins of the whole line of theological work to which I have given my life. This Project towards the specific, local and achievable appearances of the Kingdom of Justice and Shalom in the specific limited, pluralistic issues of the inner city was precisely the kind of Urban Practice that inspired me to start Urban Theology in the first place—to foster and experiment with "Theology as Action-Theology", as it was argued in *Stirrings* (Vincent, ed., 1976: 109-112).

In Urban Theology, we have always wanted to secure a place alongside both Church and Academy. It has been a determination that gave us vocational authenticity, as well as endless financial and personal crises. When asked whether UTU was part of Sheffield University, we always used to say, "No, it is part of Sheffield Inner City Ecumenical Mission". When asked whether we were the successors to Ted Wickham's Sheffield Industrial Mission (a frequent question!) we could say, "No, we are part of no denomination, and seek to live for and with all denominations—and we are rescuing the Urban from Urban-Industrial".

We thus developed a Liberation Theology style of theologising within the context of urban practice and mission. The first three UTU books of *British Liberation Theology* led in the third one to a summary of the Theology and Spirituality present in our work. Seven characteristics emerged (Rowland & Vincent, eds., 1999: 95-106):

1. *God's Realm as Presence.* The Kingdom of God realities are taking place, suddenly, in happenings, events, people, relationships, movements, projects and communities.

2. *God's Realm as Politics.* Kingdom of God constitutes breaking down boundaries, confronting powers, as unilateral initiatives, building public protests, being "pointers and prophets, rather than legislators" (98).

3. *Receiving God's Realm as a Child.* Expectations are reduced, lifestyles are downsized, to achieve the grass-roots, human, street-level, bottom-up

vulnerable character of Jesus's work and teaching, where things and people are "small".

4. *Evangelisation by the Poor.* The practitioner-theologian does not bring the Gospel, but is brought into the Gospel, through the poor and work with them. Those in need "show us the way to be human", giving us the option of an imitation of Christ in the poor.

5. *Secular Jesus Spirituality.* People act like those in the Jesus stories. Spirituality "comes from the guts of the Christ-shaped revelation in the midst of the human, from the mystery of the Body of Christ, incarnating itself at the depths of existence, where the lineaments of humanity, salvation and holiness are manifest, consumed and lived off" (102).

6. *Secularity and "en-Christedness".* "Whatever the contemporary issues of the 'secular world', whether described as 'post modern' or not, the issues of ultimacy, of Kingdom, of en-Christedness, are present." "Wherever secularity is felt at its most vicious", the Christ disciples are present, in equal secularity, "following their incarnate God" (Isaac Watts) (104).

7. *Spiritual Exercises.* Disciples develop their own "very down-to-earth rules or mottos which constitute contemporary 'spiritual exercises'." Spirituality is the 'wells' deep within each of us that sustain discernment and discipleship.

This has led us into certain "styles" of theologising, as will be clear from the stories later in the book. Kenneth Leech names seven elements (in Eastman & Latham, eds., 2004: 7-8). 1. Each small Christian community is the locus for theological activity. 2. Theological activity involves many human activities, not just intellectual. 3. A cross-section of age, class and culture is involved. 4. Theological work is an ongoing activity, involving continual interrogation, questing, struggling, wrestling. 5. Theology is messy, confronted by world, parish, neighbourhood and personal issues and crises. 6. Theology involves a prayerful, contemplative base. 7. Theology involves faith and belief.

The basis of Theology from the City is thus the actual discipleship and practice of urban Christians.

Therefore, some of the recent writings concerning urban issues written by theologians and Christian planners, sociologists and academics, will here only be referred to if their findings or insights in fact enlarge or critique what is the main burden of the book, the lived experience and the practical motivations of Christian people at work in urban areas. If there is nothing there, or nothing recorded as there, then there is no reality *from which* theology must come.

This "prejudice" in favour of a "bottom-up" approach belongs essentially to the purpose and practice of the Urban Theology Unit. I have said many times that the purpose of UTU was not to provide an urban platform for current policies, interpretations and analyses developed elsewhere by contemporary analysts, sociologists, planners or scholars in cultural studies. Rather, it was to begin to present to some of these experts, as well as to colleague practitioners and whoever else was interested, some of the practices, convictions and distinctive norms and spiritualities of some of those who work and minister in urban areas, who have found that they had to learn not only their theoretical understandings but also their theological conceptualising all over again, in order to make sense of what they find on the streets, and what they find the streets drawing out of them and their fellow disciples.

11. AN ETHNOGRAPHIC PERSPECTIVE

The theoretical approach that we are now finding most useful is the method of Ethnography. Basically, ethnography is an aspect of anthropology rather than sociology, concerned with investigating discrete, identifiable areas or groups or organisations as if they were a distinct *ethnos* (lit., nation). Ethnology is "the comparative scientific study of human peoples", and ethnography is "the scientific description of races and cultures of humankind" (*Concise Oxford Dictionary*).

So that to approach a group or activity or movement or community or church is to treat it as a separate, self-standing, unique phenomenon. The investigator therefore becomes part of the group or whatever, as far as possible, and "lives with it", and tries to describe it in the terms used by its members. Ethnography has various characteristics—participant observation, a holistic mandate, context sensitivity, socio-cultural description (Stewart, 1998: 5-7). There are some commonalities with both Grounded Theory and Naturalistic Inquiry—but they are not the same (8-10). "Truth" is the ultimate goal, despite post-modernism (12-14), with veracity, objectivity and perspicacity as its expectations (15-17). (On ethnography, see further Jenkins, ed., 2008). John Swinton says "A Hospitable and Sanctified Ethnography" suits us as it is "based on faith and choice" (in Pete Ward, ed., 2012: 71-92, 97).

The ethnographic enquirer or researcher therefore seeks to find ways of experiencing a reality from the inside, and describing it in terms recognisable to its members, if not in their words. When not a member, the researcher is a participant as well as an observer. The UTU method adds to this that the researcher is also a co-worker and thus not merely a "participant observer"—but an "observant participater." The term "auto-ethnographer" could be applied in some cases, with suitable safeguards (cf. further Roth, ed., 2005).

Similarly, Gerald West and Bongi Zengele (in Vincent, ed., 2011a: 97-105) describe how in Contextual Bible Studies, "the embodied theologies of the participants find forms of articulation" (102). The socially engaged biblical scholar and theologian work with them "to give theological form to what is already a lived reality" (103).

The researcher ideally ends up with an "inside-out" perspective, and learns to work with the "endogenous" stories and formulations and thus theologies coming from within the particular group and its life. The Endogenous perspective applies equally to the biblical theological aspects. In an Endogenous analysis of a happening or scriptural passage, we feel after the *content*, the core, the pith, what comes up from inside, which indicates the nature and motivation of the happening. This is the view *deeper into* the reality. The decisive question is: what arises from within it which bespeaks the inner spirituality, ethos, intentionality, commitment, style?

I have particularly welcomed the ethnographic method as it is a way of taking seriously the actual existing and functioning "communities" within an area—a healthy alternative to the current naïve demands from church and state that we "consider the local community", as if such a monochrome characterisation ever existed.

12. LOCATION, LOCATION, LOCATION

"Situation Analysis" has always been an essential first step in all UTU courses and work. The current document used in our MPhil/PhD course work, by Ian K. Duffield, *Contextual Analysis* (2011) gives the latest version of this, and includes the latest revision of the "Situation Analysis" document first produced by myself in 1973.

The attractive revival of theologies and spiritualities of Place (Sheldrake, 2001; Inge, 2003) has now been taken a stage further in the work of Louise Lawrence (2009). She tells contemporary stories about Christian communities working in the contexts of different places. But in each case, what "comes alive" is not simply the consciousness of locality, but also "scriptural empathies", whereby "people are enabled to 'live into' biblical texts and discover alternative visions from those (damaging ones) promoted in their contexts, hopefully to foster the Kingdom on earth". (12).

Louise Lawrence describes how four Gospel passages were used (26-38):

1. Home. Luke 15.11-32: Lost Son Homecoming.
2. Those out of Place. Luke 2. 41-52: Boy Jesus in the Temple.
3. Sustainability of Places. Luke 8.22-39: Storm-stilling and Legion.
4. The Call to be Displaced. Luke 9.46-52: Build Kingdom in other Places.

These four stories are then "worked with" in small companies of disciples in Plymouth/Devonport, in a rural village, in a fishing village, among a deaf group, and with a clergy group.

Commenting that "specific contextual readings" significantly are absent from *Faithful Cities* (48), Lawrence works with a church group of 15 in Devonport, in inner city Plymouth. Like Burngreave, it is one of Britain's 39 national multiple deprivation areas chosen for a New Deal for Communities programme. The group identified Devonport as "dissolute living" (Lk. 15.30) and "the place of pigs" (Lk. 8.32), but also saw

"Home" as the work of the Twelve's Company, a café and meeting place, "Those out of Place" as displaced adolescents, "Sustainability of Places" as providing a homecoming place, and "The Call to be Displaced" as welcoming immigrants and asylum seekers (53-59). The stories in this place also became an important part of the area's story of rebirth (59).

This is a striking example of the kind of location-specific biblical correlations which have been essential in UTU's work, as we shall see in Chapters Two and Three.

Of course, every location is a limiting, a constricting, a confinement. You can only see certain things from any one location. Indeed, what you want to see should take you to discover certain places. Laurie Green says:

> It seems to me that it is only amongst the so-called Underclass that we are to find in today's society the equivalent focus for sensitive experience, opportunity for analysis, and the comrades for symbolic/prophetic activity reminiscent of Jesus's Gospel method (Rowland & Vincent, eds., 1997: 124).

During my year as Methodist President, June 1989 to June 1990, I tried to take the inner city Christian perspectives on national issues to meetings around the country, with six lectures and meetings in the House of Commons. I developed five priorities:

- A Vision for Britain
- A Full Life for All
- Making Enterprise Common
- Local Initiatives
- Celebrating Diversity (Vincent, 1989)

Weekly returns to Sheffield inner city confirmed that their location as well as their theology was decisive in the hermeneutical circle!

13. GLOBALISATION AND THIRD SPACE

But does not every location also indicate its limitations as a standpoint, in light of globalisation? Fortunately for all readers seeking insightful interpretations of contemporary urban realities, there are several recent books by Christians which point out the importance of perspectives from globalisation (Green, 2000; Davey, 2001; Garner, 2004; *Faithful Cities*, 2006; Baker, 2009; cf. *Urban Bulletin* 2011). Here, we take that discussion for granted, and prioritise the "glocal"—the way the global is experienced in the local, in particular, in our own "local", the inner city. Even before recession hit inner cities harder than suburbs, globalisation's principal effect was that we now have "a spatial globalisation" in specific places of the *Planet of Slums* (Davis, 2006: 81-89).

Following an idea of Homi Bhabha, some theologians have attempted to describe a "Third Space", created when a local context takes on board a wider, more global, divergent perspective, and then finds an alternative space which brings elements of the new space into its understanding. In a recent volume, various theological practitioners have developed insights from this "Third Space" and their own "blurred encounters" in terms of uncongenial experiences and philosophies (Reader & Baker, eds., 2009). People, places and churches become "Hybrid" (Baker, 2009), not least with the presence of many faiths and spiritualities making "Postsecular Cities" (Baker & Beaumont, eds., 2011).

Graham and Lowe (2009: 14) observe that in Graham Ward's *Cities of God* (2000), the city is "a fragmented, atomised and deeply troubled place", but in the end "a very ethereal place", and not one relating to material issues or to the local church. Indeed, Graham and Lowe see "two different theologies of public life":

> One proceeds from a conviction that the precepts and teachings of the Christian tradition are reflected in the axioms of 'common wisdom', and that the task of the church is to commit itself to partnerships of many kinds. Alternatively, there are those who regard the Gospel as a more exclusive discourse that is designed to shape the distinctiveness of the community of faith, and to erupt prophetically into a world forgetful of transcendence and the sacred (17).

The first is labelled the way of Citizens, the second the way of Disciples. In fact, the New Testament picture of Discipleship is almost always portrayed in terms of Discipleship as Citizenship, so the difference is somewhat forced. And Graham and Lowe find themselves reluctantly questioning the Citizen's position, even though it is that of "the Anglican social tradition out of which we both write", which leads to "a more public theology by virtue of its Established nature". However, they confess:

> It may be time for the urban church to eschew the idea of 'baptising' the surrounding culture in favour of a practical theology that emphasises a more distinctive, counter-cultural, even prophetic ethic (3).

Despite this, they still hope that "historic churches" might "sit alongside the other seats of power in their cities" (141).

Urban Theology is seen by Graham and Lowe as a "Public Theology" rather than a Discipleship Theology. Here, we see it as a "Discipleship Theology" very much played out in the Public Arena, and thus as also a "Public Theology"—if the term is to be insisted upon.

Again, as against Graham and Lowe (48), my argument in the present book is that our "authority" for speaking out in public affairs does not derive either from ecclesiastical tradition (and certainly not that of bishops or Establishment, which Graham and Lowe are totally schizophrenic about!) or from "evidence-based argument" claimed as based on "local voices and experiences" (which most people would say should be voiced by the speakers, not by some outside figure to "speak out" for them).

Rather, the "authority" derives from the source of all true authority throughout Christian history—lived discipleship in a context, spoken by people (and theologians) actually doing it.

14. URBAN THEOLOGY IN DIVERSE CONTEXTS

The Urban Theology Unit has always wanted to be faithful to the limitations, the special possibilities of the urban, understood as inner city.

Consequently, my own theology cannot be the theology of other groups or individuals. I have therefore always insisted that other groups involved in liberation-style practice and theology should and must do their own "indigenous" and "endogenous" theologising. Thus, I encouraged and for four years (1976–80) worked with a group of UTU colleagues who were committed to rural ministry—work which led to the formation of the Rural Theology Association (1980). Now, I continue to theologise basically on the practice and discernments of more or less like-minded Christian practitioners, doing urban mission in contexts like my own, roughly with similar theological presuppositions. "Go for what is going for you" has always been my advice. And you can only have things "going for you" if they are actually in your experience, which is determined by your context and your life there.

As a result, I myself and all of us at UTU have worked with individuals and communities from widely differing backgrounds and orientations, helping them to develop their own individual and community theologies. Thus, many of our graduates and co-workers have themselves been supported by us to develop the present variety of urban theologies. Some fruits of this are in Chapter Three. Other groups are doing what they have learned from us and seen us do, namely take with total seriousness all the diverse elements of our racial, cultural, ethnic, locational, tradition-specific, denomination-specific environments, and discover how to do the two things which liberation practice empowers—name and fight their oppressors, and claim the Kingdom as their own.

One possibility, in the present pluralistic situation of Urban Theology, is to speak of "Urban Theologies"—different "theologies" deriving from different pieces of urban reality, so that we would speak of inner city theology, city centre theology, suburban theology, council estate theology, gated city theology, and so on.

Mario Aguilar (2008) speaks of "Liberation Theologies" in the plural, because liberation theology "has diversified to include the suffering people of God, located in many churches, many mosques, and many secular spaces." Among these, Aguilar describes theologies of inculturation, feminist and queer theologies, and ecological theologies. Urban theology itself is usually seen as belonging to the "family" of liberation theologies, if and when the conditions and methods of liberation theology are followed. It would thus be appropriate to speak of "urban theologies" if there were recognition of common bases and methods—as there is with liberation theology—which are then intentionally operated within diverse urban contexts. This is not exactly the case, at present, though there is much common methodology (e.g. Beckford, 2004).

When Urban Theology is seen as Liberation Theology, it must be because the theologising is conducted in a specific context—in this case, the urban—on the methods and by the personnel adopted by liberation theology. However, Urban Theology can be done in any urban context, without being a liberation theology. To be a liberation theology it would have to fulfil the criteria for liberation theology, namely: be based on an Option for the Poor, have its origin in an oppressed group, be motivated primarily by the biblical urges for liberation and justice, and be done by people themselves securing their own liberation by prophetic action in society. (Vincent, in Duffield, Jones & Vincent, 2000: 29-30; Laurie Green, in Rowland & Vincent, eds., 2013: 34-43). As we shall see, many of our Urban Theology stories would count also as Liberation Theology.

Chris Shannahan (2010) suggests that five British Urban Theologies exist. In fact, they are merely contextual developments of precisely our Urban Theology method: 1. Urban Liberation Theology—John Vincent, Kenneth Leech, Timothy Gorringe. "Gospel from the Borderland." 2. Urban Black Theology—Robert Beckford, Anthony Reddie, Valentina Alexander, Emmanuel Lartey, Barton Mukti, Inderjit Bhogal. "Emancipation Still Comin'." 3. Reformist Urban Theology—*Faith in the City*, *Faithful Cities*, Ann Morisy, Christopher Baker, Elaine Graham. "God is Gradual." 4. Globalisation Theology—Laurie Green, Andrew Davey. "Going Global." 5. Post-Religions Urban Theology—Gordon Lynch, Pete Ward. "Faith in a Liquid City."

Shannahan (285) concludes his study with "Seeds of a Cross-Cultural Urban Theology of Liberation", which attempts to bring together elements from 1, 2, 4 and 5, but argues for a new Hermeneutical Principle which he calls "Liberative Difference". This avoids the "theological camp mentality" of others and their "incomplete social analysis", and substitutes "the normative diversity and fluid ethnicity that characterises trans-local urbanism", resourcing "new and inclusive patterns of living and believing". "An intra-contextual 'Pentecost' of potential mutual liberation", "a new cross-cultural urban theology of liberation" which "retains a hard edge" will result. Readers will recognise that our stories of recent cross-religious activity meet some of this. However, Shannahan still works with a myth of a possible wholeness, or unity. He demands that dialogue participants must fulfil stringent criteria—express the dynamism of contemporary urban life, articulate/embody the bias to the oppressed, be committed to shared liberative struggle, be open to constructive challenge, be committed to multi-dimensional equality, and "recognise the open-endedness of struggle and the provisional status of his/her own perspective" (288).

This is a justified response to the emphasis of Baker and others on Hybridity. In the end, the hybrid is after all, a concentration of "locals". And every local is itself a unique variety of hybrid. As Sugirtharajah says (2002: 194), Hybridisation both "deflates particularisms" by "critical integration", and also "facilitates redefinitions of identities". Neither are necessarily advantageous to Endogenous Theologising, though every Hybrid produces its own "Endogenousness". And every hybrid is a developed instance of Contextual.

In the next chapter, we develop the biblical urban theological method at which we have been hinting. We conclude this chapter with a rather more down-to-earth summary of what we have seen ourselves as trying to do in our Urban Theologising.

15. THE URBAN THEOLOGISING MIX

Twenty years ago, we listed the "mix of things" in the courses which people coming to UTU would experience (Mackley, ed., 1990: 3). Ten years ago, we elaborated it in some detail (Duffield, Jones & Vincent, 2000). We reproduce the earlier version here. The original subject was "A Course at UTU". In our terms today, it is the mix of actions and investigations that go into "Urban Theologising".

First, it works with you in your context. It does not put you through psychological hoops, but it asks you to take stock of yourself—who you are, how you became it, what notions of Christianity determined your moves, what you think Christianity is about, how you view the world, and so on. Then it will ask you to study where you are—your social, economic, cultural and church context.

Second, it works with Bible models. It demands that you take seriously the variety of biblical ways of getting yourself together, sorting yourself out, and setting out in new directions. The Bible is studied (in technical terms!) inductively, experientially and experimentally.

Third, it gets you creating your own theology and understanding of the gospel and life, from your own unique point of view. We'll show you that there's plenty to choose from, plenty of "antecedents". We'll press you to become your own theologian.

Fourth, it pushes you down to deal with realities—like inner city and suburbia, rich and poor, top-down and bottom-up, oppressors and oppressed, Christians and non-Christians. You have to see where you are in all this at the same time as discovering where God and Jesus are.

Fifth, it invites you to create your own mission and vocation. If you already have one, you do a "project" within what you have. In each case, this practice embodies what you've worked at already. From it, you discover methods of "action-reflection" and "reflective-action".

Sixth, it helps you create spirituality. What "holds you together for the gospel" is our concern. We'll help you try to build up life-sustaining and action-supporting lifestyles and disciplines, interior and exterior.

So, these chapters are an attempt to issue the same kind of invitation to readers, to join in a voyage of discovery with the same kinds of interests and intentions, and hopefully leading to the same kind of results. The last two chapters indicate some specific results, in terms of mission, practice and theology, from the processes and methods described in the first two chapters.

Our aim, of course, is never "theologising" as such. "Theologising" within a context emerges as a decisive element in what became known as Contextual Theology. But, from our point of view, theologising about a situation, and/or a neighbourhood or community, and/or a Christian group, and/or oneself and a few co-practitioners, is always going to be a long process, whereby Theology informs not only one's "Reflection" on the situation or the happenings as they exist, but also informs the way those situations and happenings are interpreted (doing a Gospel Analysis of them), and crucially the way that certain aspects of them cry out for mercy or for change or for the practice of committed disciples doing some mission that is situation-relevant, gospel-inspired, community-collaborating, politically-significant and discipleship-fulfilling. The details and methods for all this are in Chapters Two and Three. Our key is that in Andrew Davey's words, "Through practice, theology has happened" (Davey, ed., 2010: ix).

16. MISSION AND VOCATION

Urban Theologising is really a Process for the discovery of Vocation and Mission, and "doing theology" is only relevant as part of that. We discovered this when from 1972 we got together our first twenty local ministers for an Urban Ministry Course, and in 1973 when we assembled our first Postgraduate Year—later re-named the Study Year or (if you wanted us to fix you with a part-time community job) the Work and Study Year.

In its most developed form, as we ran it in the 1990s, the year's process follows a routine which I here describe in the shape which we are using in a revised "Study Year" over nine weekends, based on Burngreave Ashram, which commenced in September 2010.

1. *Getting All of Myself on Board.* Everyone brings a 6-page and/or diagrammatical representation of their life so far—their personal history, background, home situation(s)—the Who, Where, What, How, When, With Whom, and Why of life so far (as in the *Journey* course, Vincent, 2001: 6-10). Everyone does a Myers-Briggs Personality Type analysis, and works with it. Once we have heard all this, we seek to clarify intentions, choices, and moves—and to identify the kind of theologies that might have informed them. Situation Analysis leads to Social Analysis and Structural Analysis (Duffield, 2011). We write a paper on "What's Coming at Me Now".

2. *Getting into the Gospel Story.* We examine the Gospel story in terms of happenings, situations, motivations and praxis (Vincent, 2009: 52-81). We seek to discern gospel situations, people and happenings that might be symbiotic with ours, and/or which might "call" us. We write a paper on

"Gospel Practice Calling Me", checking with Jesus's mission (Vincent, 2004) and "God's Project" (Rogerson & Vincent, 2009: 106-108).

3. *Creating a Response.* We dig deeper at points that seem fruitful—Gospel Models, Paradigms, People, Groupings, Geographies, Relationships, Movements. We seek to find what I can really make of the piece of earth that I have, the grasp of myself that I have, and the call of a Gospel practice that comes to me. We look at Parables, Liberation Theology, Political Theology, Feminist Theology, Black Theology, as examples. We get down in writing whatever we need from all this, using the Journey course method as guide (Vincent, 2003). We learn that arts of "Walking with the Word/Text", as Practice Interpretation describes (Vincent, ed., 2012: 1-10).

4. *Studying Models.* We visit or look up Models of others who have shared a similar context-led, gospel-drawn praxis in different times and places. Who are "our people", "our movement", "our campaign"? Who are our co-politicians, our "brothers and sisters" in the great traditions of radical praxis through radical politics, radical communities and radical discipleship? We consult a few contemporary practitioner/interpreters (Vincent, ed., 2011a) and some contemporary intentional communities (Vincent, ed., 2011b). We journal our discoveries, identifying the sources for our ongoing support and inspiration. We assemble our Jotter, our Day Book, our Library, and our Life Story.

5. *Discerning a Future Mission.* We imaginatively work out the elements of our future vocation—Who, Where, What, How, When, With Whom, Why. We project ourselves into ground plans, structures, locations, communities, fellow-disciples, books to read, trajectories to follow up, other models to relate to. Is the whole of a Gospel relevant as a "Life Line"? Mark, for instance? (Hooker & Vincent, 2010).

6. *Spirituality: Keeping All of Myself on Track.* We take ourselves in imagination and in practice, to places, people, communities, connections, networks, philosophies, study-groups that will support and provoke us in the future. We identify rules of life, discipleship disciplines, spiritualities, rituals, spaces and places that will be our "survival kit" (Ashram Community as example—Vincent, 2009).

In Chapter Two, we establish a theological base in the New Testament Dynamics of Christ, and then deal in detail with the methods that we use for Nos. 2 and 4—"Getting into the Gospel Story" and "Studying Models". The praxis of contemporary Gospel followers today thus has suggestive models from the Gospels.

In Chapter Three, we give examples of ways in which No. 5—"Future Mission" is created in the process—some "fruits" of Urban Theologising in communities and congregations, and ways in which No. 6— "Spirituality" emerges as support and inspiration.

In Chapter Four, we survey the current Urban scene, and the ways it is being interpreted, to see what our methods and their results add up to politically and strategically for Church and Nation.

Chapter Two

THE DYNAMICS

OF CHRIST

1. THE DYNAMICS OF CHRIST

I first outlined the concept of the Dynamics of Christ in *Secular Christ* in 1968, partly provoked by Harvey Cox. In *Secular City* (1965), the Church's Kerygma function becomes "broadcasting the seizure of power", its Diakonia function is "Healing the Urban Fractures", and its Koinonia function "Making Visible the City of Humanity". This seemed a promising start. But these identifications are not proved either from a theological or a sociological point of view. The Kingdom which "still occurs" is merely the city. The christological categories have no distinctive value or relevance.

That conclusion pointed up the exciting possibilities for a theology of God's action in history and society which would be more closely based on the actions of God in Christ, and which would seek to discern the techniques whereby God may be assumed to be still working as in the Christ-deeds in the New Testament. This would mean careful and patient experimentations with the Christological categories and Gospel stories within the various areas of modern secular existence, to delineate the actions of the "dynamic Christ" who is our contemporary now. The dynamics of Christ's action in the world now grow thus from New Testament insights, as I outlined in *Secular Christ* (156-158, 227-228):

1. *All things made by Christ* (John 1.3, Col. 1.16) points to the way of *Christology* and the dynamics of Christ in human existence, as the new being of humanity foreshadowed in Jesus.

2. *All things found in Christ* (1 Cor. 15. 22, John 1.4, 2 Cor. 5. 18-19, Col. 3.11) points to the way of *healing* and the dynamics of Christ in human morality, as the "new morality" of the Kingdom.

3. *All things held together in Christ* (Col. 1.17, 2.10, Heb. 1.3, Eph. 1.10) points to the way of *hiddenness* and to the dynamics of Christ in society, as the inner presence of the issues of discipleship within secular situations and issues.

4. *All things find their end in Christ*, (1 Cor. 15.24, 28, Heb. 1.2, Col. 3. 11) points to the way of *political practice* and to the dynamics of Christ in history, as a way whereby the techniques of identification and transformation operate in historical events.

5. *All things are yours* (1 Cor. 3. 22-23, Col. 1. 21-23, 3.3) points to the gift of *significance and wholeness*, as an inner supportive spirituality.

These perspectives based on non-Synoptic sources in the New Testament obviously need to be filled out by reference to the specific ways in which the first three Gospels describe the actions and words of Jesus. In what ways do the Gospels suggest attitudes, strategies, and disciplines, which produced Christ-style practice in the first disciples, which might then be adapted by modern disciples seeking to follow and look for and even precipitate similar dynamics in their own contexts today?

That question can only be dealt with by detailed work with the Synoptic Gospels. To that we now turn.

2. MOVING INTO THE TEXT

Our Urban Theology's method is thus to work with urban realities and with urban people towards their own transformation, based upon and taking its inspiration from the biblical model of the praxis of an urban Jesus, working towards the transformation of society and people in urban Galilee.

In *The City in Biblical Perspective* (Rogerson & Vincent, 2009) I indicate how, recently, many scholars and archaeologists have established the essentially urban character of Galilee in the time of Jesus. Jesus's practice, his activity, in the midst of that context, is clear. Jesus, in a word, seeks to establish small urban/rural settlement mini-communities of reciprocity, commonness and intentionality. The scenarios of Jesus in the Gospels are vital as the lifeblood of this Kingdom-on-earth dynamic which Jesus establishes.

The key aspect of this God's Realm/Kingdom-centred praxis of Jesus is that the work itself generates and is carried along by specific projects which manifest and carry out specific items in the transformative agenda.

As Ian Wallis says, Mark "helps us to discover Jesus in our own Galilees" (in Vincent, ed., 2006: 191). Modern urban disciples often see their presence in an urban area as a response to a call from Jesus. It seems to them that there are so many ways in which the inner city or housing estate are "like" the urban villages of Galilee. They have the same feeling and ethos, as well as similar economic, social and political indicators. An "Urban Hearing for the Gospel" (Vincent, 1997) has been experienced. "Will you come and follow me?" has often been the origin of their being in this place. They study the Gospel story and their modern urban experience, and declare, "This is That" (Acts. 2.16) (*Faithfulness in the City*, 2003: 216-220; Vincent, ed., 2012: 7). They are "engaging with the texts in the context of commitment and action" (Christopher Rowland in Vincent, ed., 2006: 5).

Once in a context in which they feel Jesus is at home, the urban disciples look to aspects of Jesus's life and ministry as a guide to what they might be like, or how they might relate, or what they might do. They find themselves alongside others who in practice if not in word are saying "Be imitators of me as I am of Christ" (I Cor. 11.1) (Rogerson & Vincent, 2009: 80). They conclude: "What we are struggling to understand and embody are the contours of the *character* of Christ, as Phil. 2.6-11 indicates" (Rowland & Roberts, 2008: 22).

Urban disciples, then, instinctively "make connections" between biblical stories, especially stories from Jesus and the Gospels, and their own contemporary stories coming from their environment, their experiences and their projects.

The Bible does not offer extractable 'answers' to modern-day questions, but rather lived examples of interpretation in action; that is, a record of the hermeneutical methods that Jesus, Paul, Peter and others deployed in the specific human situations in which they found themselves (Rowland & Roberts, 2008: 21).

In *The City in Biblical Perspective*, we indicate a developed method for situation and practice correlation between scriptural contexts and contemporary contexts. The biblical methodology we employ is best illustrated in the three-fold scheme which Norman Gottwald developed for use in the UTU/New York Theological Seminary Doctor of Ministry programme. It features a three-stage process:

1. The Move from My Situation to the Text
2. The Movement within the Text (Exegesis proper)
3. The Move from the Text's Movement back to my Situation
(Gottwald, in Vincent, 2006: 15-17; Rogerson & Vincent, 2009: 105-108)

Another *genre* to which this method belongs is that known as *Sachkritik*, which aims not at "retrieving an original meaning", but rather at discovering "relationships": This "contextually driven reading" works by "mutual dialogue".

> The reader seeks understanding in the relationship between his or her situation—biographical, political, social—and the text itself. The text illuminates the world of the reader, the world of the reader illuminates the meaning of the text (Rowland & Roberts, 2008: 108).

Constantly, the warning of Norman Gottwald has to be recalled:

> Am I prepared to abandon a false or abortive start when the text or theme or biblical period do not speak to the problem that I first thought they did? (Gottwald, in Vincent, 2006: 16. Also in Rogerson & Vincent, 2009: 105)

In terms of present-day theological writings, one contribution of the present work is to set before colleagues in several disciplines, the interpretative methods between scripture and practice with which we have experimented, and a few of the theological learnings towards which we have found ourselves being drawn in the last decade or so, following these methods.

Two elements are primary. First, a Gospel Situation Analysis. Second, a Gospel Practice Analysis.

3. A GOSPEL SITUATION ANALYSIS

So, then, what might a Situation Analysis of Jesus in his time look like?

This can be learned from the Gospel stories. We learn about the situation as it was, partly because Jesus's Realm/Kingdom/Will of God present on earth relates to the then established societal and political realities, and partly because Jesus's Realm constitutes an Alternative City described often in terminology coming from the established realities (Vincent, 2004: 74-80; Rogerson & Vincent, 2009: 62-65, 69-70). Each situational aspect may thus be named alongside its Jesus-sourced opposite.

1. Judaism has a political and municipal system based on a divinely-provided legal code, administered by hereditary officers. Jesus's alternative city is one determined by human love, the imitation of a divine "father", and constitutes a subversion of Judaism. This free society of equals thus represents a new civic body of radical humanism and secularism. Politics is transformed.

2. Rome's city embodies domination, paternalism and the power of force. Jesus's alternative city embodies lordship based on servanthood, the rejection of imperial authorities by each being the servant of the other, and by the elevation of women. This is a subversion of the Roman system, and represents a new civic reality of egalitarianism, sexual equality and "levelling". Marginalisation is reversed. Society is transformed.

3. Possession of land, wealth, and appointment determine the social and economic system. Jesus substitutes a realm in which the poor, the disabled, the excluded, the little ones, the children, are elevated. The privileged are thus subverted. This represents a force of radical reversals, of an "upside down" Kingdom. Relationships are transformed.

4. Power is held by elites—Priests, Sanhedrin, Kings, office bearers. Jesus substitutes those outside all elites, including not only those on the edges of Judaism unable to fulfil the Torah, but finally those completely outside Judaism. A new "hierarchy"—the twelve tribal heads of Galilean fishermen and traders—subverts the office-bearers and post-holders. Sacredness, honour and proper role are thus transformed. "The little tradition" (Gorringe, 2002: 8-9), "hidden transcripts" (Horsley, 2008: 16-17), "the people's history" (Horsley, 2010: 1-20) "the lesser traditions" (Green, 2010b: 108) get empowered.

Following the lines of this four-fold agenda in politics, society, relationships and hierarchies, the contemporary disciple then moves beyond "Making Connections" to a wider perspective, a perspective of "God's Project". A particular passage, theme or word may resonate with a contemporary situation or happening, but that may be purely coincidental, or marginal to the issue, or even a matter of personal perception. A larger question must now also be asked: How does our situation or story not only evoke a Gospel resonance, but also cohere with the larger perspective of the Gospel, what we might call "The Whole Project of Jesus", or "God's Project"?

In *The City in Biblical Perspective*, I consider the particular contributions of the four Gospels separately in relation to both these questions (Vincent, 2009: 72-79, 96-101). With what particular events or missions or leadings does a particular Gospel invite its readers to identify, and then use as a model for their practice?

In each case, I observe the move from specific identification to the wider level:

There is always a second level, where the citizen/disciple moves beyond a ministry to the needy individual or group in their situation, and seeks to bring change to the wider context of people and institutions in the city (80).

This is developed in a systematic model for "Moving from Connections" to "Securing Coherence with God's Project" (104-107).

Each stage or aspect of a typical Gospel story is now projected further into more global policy. We thus end (80-81) with a model of a series of "Immediate Identifications" of elements in a Gospel Encounter, which lead on to a "Wider Practice" of Elements of Jesus/God's Project. This can be developed as two inter-related strategies; in which immediate identifications are "Acted Parables" of "Wider Practice":

I. Immediate Identifications from the Gospel Encounter	II. Wider Practice for the Project of God/Jesus
1. Person addressed	1. Oppressor addressed
2. Situation dealt with	2. Social situation dealt with
3. Sufferer healed	3. Fellow sufferers healed
4. New life for individual	4. New life for group
5. New future for individual	5. New future for class or group
6. New community	6. New communities
7. Victimising power challenged	7. Wider controllers tackled
8. Critics rebuffed	8. Structures subverted

4. A GOSPEL PRACTICE ANALYSIS

Some ways of getting a Gospel analysis to work in our own situation is basic to our whole enterprise. A "Dynamics of Christ" Theology from the City is a theology of continuing Christo-praxis Discipleship, a following of the Incarnate One in the midst of specific places and activities in the *human zone* in which it seems most at home. It is a theology of process, inasmuch as the initial immersement or "inmundation" is a non-repeatable and decisive movement. It is an "in-mundus." movement, a movement into the world, the *mundus*, rather than an "in-carnis" movement, a movement into the *carnis,* the flesh. It is a flowering of the charisms of Christ-likeness and Christ-imitation in the individual—an enormous expansion of the *persona* to assimilate to the spirit of Jesus, but in the individual as part of secular reality, *mundus* reality, manifest not in interior spirituality or consciousness, but in holistic humanness and action.

Yet it is also a constricting, a concentration, a whittling-down, of the individual disciple's *persona*, to achieve at least in intention the "one thing needful", notably the submission of the self to the restrictions, disciplines and limitations of the singular location and the particular relevant vocation. Such "immersement" is thus both an expansion of self to fill a Christ-space, and a restriction of self to allow only what is now needed. It is both a "Losing Life", and a "Gaining Life" (cf. Vincent, ed., 2006: 68-78).

Our practice therefore has to take very seriously and by differentiations and discernments the Gospel elements to which we are really being called, plus those elements necessary actually to fulfil that calling, and even those elements unavoidably or intentionally left out.

In fact, all Urban Theologians discover their own "Canon within the Canon". There are often common biblical themes. Colin Marchant names Incarnation, Servant, Shalom and Kingdom, plus special "themes that resonate in the urban today", named as the value of the individual in the image of God, the divine preference for the poor, the need for justice, jubilee and liberation, and wrestling with principalities and powers (in Eastman & Latham, eds., 2004: 8-11).

All this underlines the importance of bringing some kind of alternative analysis into the situation. All that we have learned of Jesus Christ and his "Kingdom of God on earth", and of the early Christian communities creating a "third estate", invites us to consider what perspectives might be possible from these sources, from this "Density of Presence" (Davey in Davey, ed., 2010: 84-96).

The Gospel Situation Analysis and Practice Analysis of Jesus imply that also today, we need a genuine View from Below. What are the *effects* of current arrangements on those at the bottom of society? What analyses exist of the present situation? If we compare *A Petition of Distress from the Cities* (1993), how far are the equivalents of the characteristics of exclusion, poverty, education, community, race, young people, transport, housing and homelessness—and of Government policies—present in Jesus's Galilee? What evocations occur—both ways? To this we shall constantly return.

5. MARKS OF THE GOSPEL

Steven Croft sees a fundamental call to Church today to be "Jesus' People" (Croft, 2009). He outlines many strategies for contemporary followers of Christ, based upon the identification of aspects of Jesus's practice which are possible and relevant for disciples today.

Urban practitioners and theologians need to develop a sophisticated use of Gospel Criteria. What perspectives are suggested by Gospel texts? A list of frequently used passages constitutes an inner city mission "canon" of leading overall perspectives:

Mark 1.14-15	The Presence of the Realm of God
Mark 1.16-20	Call of Disciples
Mark 4.2-8, 26-29	Sower and Growth of Seeds
Luke 1.47-55	Magnificat of the Oppressed
Luke 4.17-18	The Jubilee Declaration
Luke 14.15-21	The Great Feast

(See further Vincent, 2000: 181-183)

All this can be seen as the Jubilee brought by Jesus—as I argue in the article, "Jesus and Jubilee" (in Rogerson, ed., 2013). In the Jubilee of Jesus, the previously marginalised are brought in, and others become marginalised. Crucial questions have to be: Who *gains* from this Gospel activity? Who *loses* from it? In Gospel analysis terms, this constitutes specific aspects of Jesus's practice which give us "Marks" of the Gospel. The question of "winners" and "losers" can be pursued by means of imagining a list of "marks" or "distinctive traits" in the Gospel, and charting their effects on different persons and groups:

MARKS OF JESUS / GOSPEL	"WINNERS"	"LOSERS"
1. Commitment and discipleship to Jesus	Disciples	Non-Disciples
2. Vulnerability, openness to being used	Servants	Dominators
3. Supportive group being created	The Twelve	Previous Heads
4. Reversal of human values/expectations	Those who see	"The blind"
5. People changing life-styles	Give up all	The left behind
6. Division because of Jesus	Disciple "family"	Prior families
7. The mighty brought down	The Oppressed	Authorities
8. People being crucified	Jesus, The Twelve	Rulers
9. Crucified people being raised up	Jesus, Paul	Priests

10. Religious authorities disempowered	Challengers	Scribes, Pharisees
11. Political authorities subverted	The Excluded	Romans
12. Outcasts welcomed at banquets	Publicans, Sinners	Torah-faithful
13. Foreigners within the Kingdom	Gentiles	Judaic faithful
		(Earlier version in Vincent, 1983:14)

Once discerned, the Gospel Marks become significant also as directing us to hints for further stages in our method. First, the "winners" continue their characteristic persons, activities and missions through the activities of the Christian community. Second, the "losers" are identifiably continuing in the "principalities and powers", the structures and authorities of political power and societal norms.

ACTIONS OF JESUS / GOSPEL "Marks"	DISCIPLE GROUP PRACTICES & PROJECTS "Winners"	POLITICAL & SOCIETAL POWERS & LAWS "Losers"

The Christian Group Practices and Projects are in Chapter Three. The Political, Societal and State "outworkings" are in Chapter Four.

6. THE JESUS PRAXIS CYCLE

A theological method, a "hermeneutic", derives from this and seeks to enable it. Liberation Theology has produced many versions of the "Hermeneutical Circle". A better title is "Hermeneutical Cycle", as each circle leads on to another. The concept of the "Circle" or "Cycle" is in fact now a familiar one in many varieties of contemporary theology. Basically, "hermeneutical" indicates "how meaning (*hermeneia*) is conveyed or proceeded with". So a hermeneutical circle or cycle suggests how you get from one thing to another.

As I have endlessly worked at this, I have found it a useful way to discover how we can "do theology". In practice, everyone should work out their own "circle/cycle". For myself, it has seemed to me that the Gospel pattern of Jesus's way of dealing with people and situations suggests its own circle and cycle (Vincent, ed., 2006: 11-14). The model of Jesus engaged in mission, as described in the Gospels, provides a very distinctive "circle" or "cycle".

1. *Jesus Sees*: Jesus is described as *seeing* some individual or group or situation with a need or a problem or an unacceptable circumstance.

2. *Jesus Loves*: Jesus takes account of the person and situation; and he "is filled with compassion". His *heart* goes out in love towards the person or group in need.

3. *Jesus Acts*: Jesus holds out his *hands* in healing or assistance or exorcism, or he seeks to act in some other way to remedy the situation, or he calls the person to act or do something.

4. *Jesus Plans*: Jesus's *head* is engaged as he addresses in a rational way the restrictions of the context surrounding the position occupied by the individual or group.

5. *Jesus Envisages*: Jesus holds out a new future for the person. The individual or group's future or "project" or practice is described—what their "following Jesus" is to entail in their life thereafter.

6. *Jesus Empowers:* Jesus empowers or constructs Kingdom-style political alternatives, especially related to allies (Community) and authorities (Politics).

7. *Jesus Theologises*: Jesus proclaims the significance of what has happened, often in response to critics. Elements of a "theology" thus are concluded.

The Jesus Cycle thus goes:

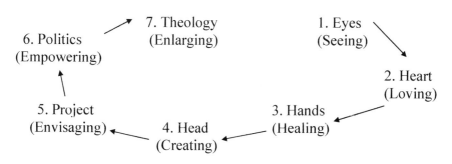

Cutely, Laurie Green sees Jesus as acting on our UTU model:

With Jesus, theological reflection offers critique, offers an alternative, and demands change—and all this only after thirty years of situation analysis (Green, 2003: 82).

Green observes how Jesus projects "a new culture, a new way of being, a new logic, a new society whose participants will change the world radically" (82). Indeed, the Jesus Cycle tells us how to "change the world radically" in the way that Jesus changed it.

7. THE JESUS VOCATIONAL CYCLE

Jesus's own Vocation can also be understood as a Circle or Cycle, following the seven elements of Jesus's praxis cycle.

First, there is *Incarnation*. He begins from outside—from God (Jn. 1, Phil. 2), or from a human home (Luke and Matthew), or from Galilee (Mark). He becomes "incarnate", in the world, in history, in a particular time and place, is anointed in baptism to perform his mission and vocation, faces temptation to deny it, and then immerses himself in it.

Second, for Jesus, there is *Proclamation*. Jesus begins his ministry by proclaiming the presence now on earth, in time, of the Realm/Kingdom of God (Mk. 1.14), the Year of Jubilee (Lk. 4.18-19). He declares the purpose of his calling and the nature of his practice as to celebrate and to extend God's Realm, God's will, on earth.

Third, there is *Identification*. Jesus's Mission is especially to the people outside of normal Judaism, with its Synagogue, Law and Temple. He goes rather to find the demon-possessed (Mk. 1.21-34), the publicans and law-breakers (Mk. 2.13-17), the poor, crippled, blind and lame (Lk. 14.13, 21). These are the people with whom he identifies, to whom he journeys downwards, and for whom he brings wholeness.

Fourth, Jesus inaugurates a *Movement*. He becomes the champion of the dispossessed (Mk. 2.17). He embodies the values of the dispossessed (Mk. 2.13-17). He celebrates his Messianic Banquet with the dispossessed (Lk. 4.7-25). He makes his disciples become one with the dispossessed—hence the Beatitudes (Lk. 6.20-23).

Fifth, Jesus creates a *Community* to carry forward his own practice and to repeat the cycle of Incarnation, Proclamation, Identification and Movement development. The Twelve are a micro-praxis, enabling model for the Community, in Task (Mk. 3.14), Constitution (Mk. 3.33-35), Mission (Mk. 6.6-13) and Significance (Mk. 10.28-31).

Sixth, Jesus relates to the reality of his work for the wider world (Mk. 2.17, 3.4-6, 3.22-26). He produces elements of stances within *Society and Politics*.

Seventh, Jesus expands upon the total significance of his Practice as a basis for an alternative *Faith and Theology*—and is represented by Gospel writers as doing so. Early instances in Mark are 1.34, 2.10, 2.17, 2.27-28.

Thus, there is a Jesus Vocational Cycle. Jesus moves from being the Presence of God's Realm (Incarnation), on to Proclaiming the reality of God's Realm (Proclamation), on to siding with the special beneficiaries of God's Realm (Identification), then to creating an alternative movement to extend God's Realm (Movement), with a necessary supportive and continuing grouping (Community), and a newly empowered activity and attitude towards authorities (Politics), all of which constitutes new truth for the world (Theology).

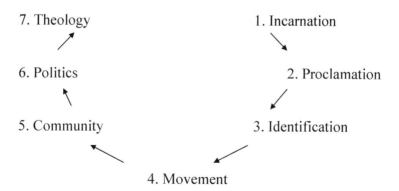

The Two Jesus Cycles constitute the "Dynamics of Christ", as I hinted at and hoped for in *Secular Christ* (Vincent, 1968: 181-195).

8. THE DISCIPLESHIP CYCLE

The Discipleship Vocational Cycle follows the model of the Jesus Vocational Cycle, and extends it. Our discipleship often has to take its cue from the model of Jesus in Incarnation. Thus, we may say that we also have to begin with self-realisation within or movement into our context—Orientation. Then we have to move on to radical new discoveries along the lines of Jesus's own ministry, which serve as a spur, a challenge, to us—Provocation. That means we have to sort out our lives in the light of what is being revealed, and find the places, people and causes appropriate to it—Identification. Then, we too have to become part of Jesus's practice and create some practical response, we have to participate in what he is doing—Movement. The Community is necessary to keep the Discipleship Cycle going—but it must never be an end in itself. The practical manifestation in the world relates to Society and the State—Politics. Theology is the explication of the Dynamic Cycle in all its implications.

However, there seem to be people in church and world today who are apparently blind, who seemingly never see any people in need. Two prior tactics are needed. The Seeing–Loving–Handling–Creating cycle is fine for those who are in the place or with the people where their experiences or encounters can now evoke radical response, for those who are already in a place where they are "incarnate". Others have to get there first.

So for them, two additions to the "circle" are necessary. The "seeing" as perceiving and being deeply conscious of realities only comes after one has gone out of one's way and encountered people and situations which are initially totally unfamiliar. It is a "Crossover" (Laurie Green, in Davey, ed., 2010: 11-12), probably a "Journey Downwards".

The Jesus Discipleship Cycle therefore brings in two decisive new elements. A disciple first has to make the decision to follow in the Jesus Way, i.e. move the feet. Then, second, a disciple has to become part of the movement's community, learn to share in parts of the common life, i.e., engage the stomach! So the Jesus Discipleship Full Circle goes:

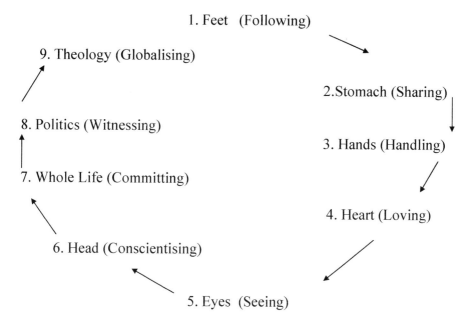

1. Feet   (Following)

9. Theology (Globalising)

2.Stomach (Sharing)

8. Politics (Witnessing)

3. Hands (Handling)

7. Whole Life (Committing)

4. Heart (Loving)

6. Head (Conscientising)

5. Eyes (Seeing)

This can be expressed in the "upside down" image, plotting a discipleship progress through "stages" of personal involvement in the order of the discipleship stories in Mark (Vincent, 2001: 18-19; 2007:12-15):

1. FEET: First, follow (Mk. 1.13-17)
2. STOMACH: Then come for a meal (Mk. 2.13-17)
3. HANDS: Then, share in the action (Mk. 6.7-13)
4. HEART: Then, have compassion (Mk. 6.36-46)
5. EYES & EARS; Then, perceive realities (Mk. 8.18)
6. HEAD: Then, say who I am (Mk. 8.27-30)
7. WHOLE LIFE: Thus, find life (Mk. 8.34-37)
8. POLITICS: Relate to the Powers (Mk. 9.30-32)
9. FULFILMENT: Finally, get everything
    (Mk. 10.28-31)

The need for this "upside down" discipleship plan has come from my experience with dozens of people who, over the years, have expressed interest in Christian discipleship. But often it leads nowhere. They ask endless questions, but they are all theoretical. In reality, explanation, persuasion, argument are only needed after people have been prepared to take some steps into the unknown—to begin to follow. Often, only when they have discovered a new place (feet), and shared the lives of new people and new realities (stomach), and only when they have rediscovered themselves doing different things with these new places and people (hands), will they become moved (heart) and enlightened/converted (eyes) and "come to themselves" (head), and experience the new reality as a whole (life), which reorientates them in society (politics), and which they then see as a totally new reality—a hundredfold around them (fulfilment).

Our "theological practice" of the "discipleship cycle" is based upon an "Imitation" of the practice of Jesus. Jesus does not initially ask people to believe in him with their head. He does not even initially invite people to love him with their heart. Jesus first of all invites people to follow him with their feet, and then share a common life. Heart and head become engaged where the feet have taken them, and with those with whom the move has landed them. All the mysteries of life and fulfilment only apply within and after these first practices, which could be a Journey Downwards. To act on this is what "Faith" is.

Our UTU "Study Year" from 1973 to 1997 each year provided for 10–20 people of all ages just such an experience of involvement, which led to theological and vocational reconstruction (Vincent, 1982: 47-50; Mackley, 1990: 5, 16, 26-29).

9. GOSPEL CYCLES IN PRACTICE

Once people have become disciples, they then become involved in the Jesus Missional activity ("Project"), and thus themselves join in what I have described as the Jesus Praxis Cycle. Out of all this, new community and politics are created, and new understanding or "truth" emerges—out of all this, "theology" is born or reborn.

In fact, this is not unlike the classic Hermeneutical Circle of South American Liberation Theology, of See, Judge, Act (see Boff & Boff, 1989: 24-42) with the addition of the initial stages of becoming aware of God's Call and joining the Community, and the subsequent stages of Project and Theology.

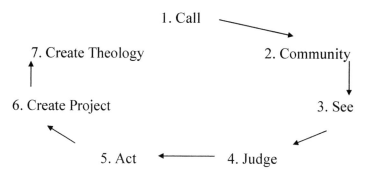

1. Call

7. Create Theology   2. Community

6. Create Project   3. See

5. Act   4. Judge

Laurie Green has produced a rather more discursive reflective model of a Hermeneutical Cycle, which could be compared to our method here. Laurie's goes:

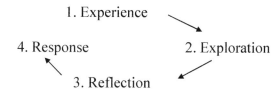

1. Experience

4. Response   2. Exploration

3. Reflection

Laurie Green's book *Let's Do Theology* (Green, 1990, rev. 2009) provides a philosophical and extended argument for this kind of method. Here, I am more concerned to give a working tool for vocation and mission, issuing in more specific lines to follow in terms of a project.

My own experience in working with the Hermeneutical Cycle has been in courses of the Urban Theology Unit—the Urban Ministry Course (1971– 97), the Study Year (1973–1997), the Doctor of Ministry Course of the New York Theological Seminary (1978–1990), the Diploma in Theology and Mission Course (1978–1997), the Master and Bachelor Degrees in Ministry and Theology (1992–2000), the Diploma in Community Ministry Course (1985–1998) the PhD Courses in Urban, Contextual and Liberation Theologies (Sheffield and Birmingham Universities, 1991 to present), and the MA/PGDip in Theology (York St. John University, 2000–2012), especially the MA/PGDip in Urban Theology (2005–2011) with Modules on Urban Context in Contemporary Britain, Urban Theology and Bible, Theologies of Liberation, and Theology and Local Communities.

In each, we have developed various different process methodologies.

Each seeks to move people from analysis of their context, through to discernment of a crucial issue, problem or injustice (1. See). People's context may have changed because of their "Journey Downwards" or "Crossover" (p.60 above) – what Liberation Theology calls "Making an Option for the Poor". This often leads to a conversion-style "coming to new sight" from a new experience-based "perception of scandals" (Boff & Boff, 1989, 2). "Scandals" are the realities of human deprivation, marginalisation or injustice, perceived in the light of the Marks of the Gospel, and especially Christ's presence in the poor (Matt. 25. 31-46).

From this we seek methods of research and commitment focussing on the "scandal", using biblical and other antecedents, especially relevant Scriptural Models for Mission/Project (2. Judge). This in turn leads on to designing, setting up and carrying out a relevant Project (3. Act). The Project then is critiqued, celebrated and globalised (4. Expand), critically reviewed in light of the original concern and the learnings reaped for new understanding (5. Recreate), and finally taken back into the context, by then hopefully changed.

This gives us the "Urban Theology Hermeneutical Circle" which leads on to a further Cycle based on the new situation (6. Next Circle).

So, the developed Urban Theology Hermeneutical Cycle looks like this:

URBAN THEOLOGY
HERMENEUTICAL CYCLE

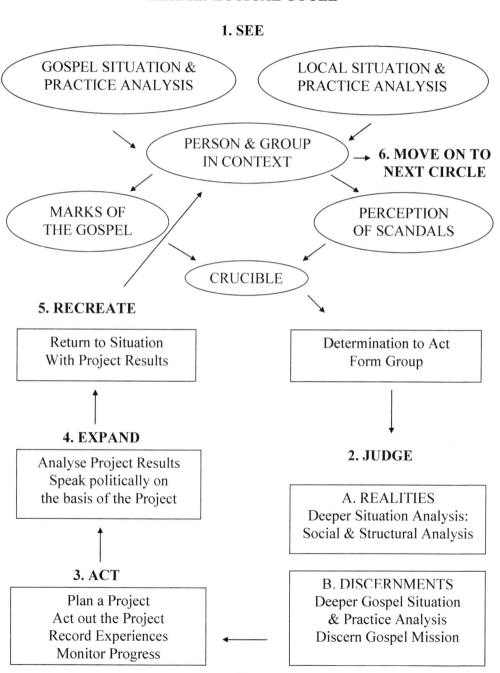

1. SEE

GOSPEL SITUATION &
PRACTICE ANALYSIS

LOCAL SITUATION &
PRACTICE ANALYSIS

PERSON & GROUP
IN CONTEXT

6. MOVE ON TO
NEXT CIRCLE

MARKS OF
THE GOSPEL

PERCEPTION
OF SCANDALS

CRUCIBLE

5. RECREATE

Return to Situation
With Project Results

Determination to Act
Form Group

4. EXPAND

Analyse Project Results
Speak politically on
the basis of the Project

2. JUDGE

A. REALITIES
Deeper Situation Analysis:
Social & Structural Analysis

3. ACT

Plan a Project
Act out the Project
Record Experiences
Monitor Progress

B. DISCERNMENTS
Deeper Gospel Situation
& Practice Analysis
Discern Gospel Mission

10. CRUCIBLE

An image we have often used in our work is that of the Crucible. I first used it in print in 1983 in an article called "Towards an Urban Theology" (Vincent, 1983). It was regularly used in the DMin courses of 1978–1989 and was later used by Laurie Green (2000: 102; 2010: 85).

The idea of the Crucible is that the process of urban theologising brings together gospel and situation elements into a white-hot "mix", a cauldron, a crucible, out of which the pure metal of Christ-faithful and situation-faithful practice and project come.

Partly, this is asking the Situation question of the Gospel Marks, and asking the Gospel Marks question of the Situation. In each case, we are not dealing with some global generalisation, but always with some specific, limited, stories or marks or aspects of Gospel and of Situation, and seeing whether there is a fruitful interaction or "snap". Thus we ask:
- Gospel Marks—Where are the Gospel Bits in our Situation Marks?
- Situation Marks—Where are our Situation Bits in the Gospel Marks?

The Situation characteristics and the Gospel characteristics are both subjected to this kind of questioning in turn, to begin to get the feel of contrary elements and possible identifications. Then we bring bits of the Gospel and bits of the Situation into critical dialogue in order to push them together into a "crucible". Here we are engaged in a dynamic interplay, where conflict, values, assessments and perceptions are keenly felt.

Elements and stories are "pluralistic", both at the Gospel end and at the Situation end. It will be only "bits" of that pluralistic Gospel situation which will spark off "bits" of the pluralistic contemporary situation. Thus:

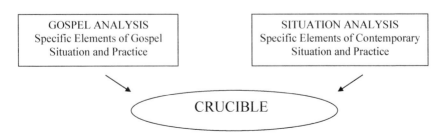

| GOSPEL ANALYSIS Specific Elements of Gospel Situation and Practice | SITUATION ANALYSIS Specific Elements of Contemporary Situation and Practice |

CRUCIBLE

Hence, in the Crucible, there is a battle and a resolution between elements from the Gospel and elements from the Situation. We are asking questions like: Which one or two bits of Gospel seem to "snap" with one or two bits of Situation? What other bits of Gospel seem to be at odds with other bits of Situation?

11. PROJECT

From here, we begin to get the sense of some call, or action, or mission. Here, the "penny drops" and discernment occurs. The dynamic, conflictual factors lead to something new—which combines elements of Situation and Gospel. So we need to know: (1.) Which bits of Situation could be tackled on any grounds? (2.) Which bits of Situation could only be tackled on Gospel grounds? 3. What priority comes from the Gospel bit(s)? (4.) What priority comes from the Situation bit(s)? In other words, we start discussing what is going to happen anyway; what will only happen if we do something; and what it is possible for us to do. From this, the practitioner and the church group get a hint of a "possible hope", of a project, a piece of mission or strategy which then has to be worked through with others.

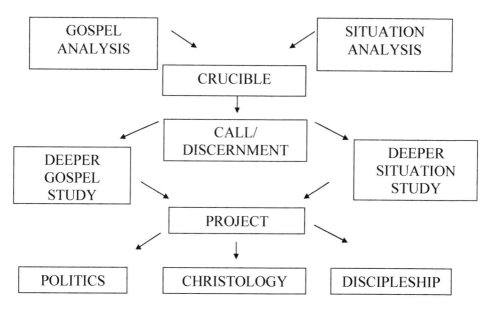

Basically, the Project seeks to continue and be consistent with the Project of Jesus—to set up, embody, and sustain responses to current situations and persons which constitute manifestations of the Messianic work of Jesus to set up and constitute the Realm/Kingdom/Commonwealth of God.

In the three Sections which follow, we press the three areas of Politics, Christology and Discipleship in so far as they relate to and have specificity and dynamic from these three elements as characterised in the Gospels. They each raise criteria, characteristics and marks of Jesus Kingdom-practice in the respective areas.

We will indicate some results of this whole process in the next chapter. The criteria and working models from the Gospel dynamics emerge and develop especially in three areas of Gospel insights—in Politics, in Christology, and in Discipleship.

From this point on, our work at UTU has been with practitioners, community workers, ministers and theologians who want to discipline their practice, or provoke new practice, with this dynamic in mind. In some cases this has developed in response to specific problems, issues or challenges within the student's own context, so that methods of critical discernment and elaboration have been developed. Part of a recent document by Ian K Duffield on Project Proposal Identification points up three areas for work:

1. *Social, Political, Economic and Psychological Factors.* In what way is this a problem which demands systemic change, addressing causes as well as symptoms? What social, political, economic, and psychological factors contribute to this problem? Specifically indicate the nature and structure of sexism, racism, and/or classism as these affect your problem concerns.

2. *Biblical and Missional Factors.* a) How does the problem and issues it raises, along with sensed possibilities for change, relate to the biblical tradition? i.) in terms of the "grand design" in scripture? ii.) in terms of specific "calls" from individual passages/stories/personalities? b) What is the discernment in the Site Team and Candidate of the vital areas and issues in mission which are involved in the situation and the problem to be addressed?

3. *Research.* a) What do you need to know in order to shed light on the problem? b) What areas of research may you need to explore later on? c) What critical questions are being raised for you? d) Identify possible biblical antecedents, theological resonances, historical parallels to your situation and the problem you are addressing.

12. POLITICS

The "Project" in the Urban Theology Cycle, coming out of the Crucible, will often be in the realms of community and politics as the "Wider Practice" (p. 53 above). The New Testament in its own contexts in fact encourages at least four different overall models for "Making Connections" and "Securing Coherence with God's Project" in society as a whole. Each of them suggests different implications for urban practice today.

1. *Jesus: Embodiment.* Jesus embodies the values and life of God's Realm, God's Will, here on earth. He thus represents an "Alternative Reality" which implies both an alternative personal existence and also an alternative community of mutuality and project which comprises an Alternative City. In light of this, the fundamental calling of the Christian community is to be a relevant, secular, embodied manifestation on the streets of the new reality present on earth, the Realm/Kingdom of God. So, we engineer

- Unilateral Initiative

2. *Jesus: Subversion.* Jesus evades the question of choosing between Rome and Temple in Mark 12.13-17, and thus subverts both. The task in the city today, then, on this view, is to find ways to embody a politics and a community which as far as possible keeps us out of unnecessary trouble but inwardly subverts the authorities, tries to pioneer an alternative society, and meanwhile allows us to live differently. So, we set up

- Acted Parables

3. *Paul: Compliance.* Romans 13 encourages obedience, or at least compliance, to the state, though Paul is not consistent. On this model, Christians in the city comply with civic laws without questioning them. But this has only worked when Christians could connive with a powerful

state, not when the state persecuted them or made impossible their alternative project(s). So many today see Paul as representing "critical solidarity", whereby Christians live exemplary lives though not in politics as citizens. So, we get not necessarily "counter-culture", but probably

- Counter-Contextuality

4. *Revelation: Replacement.* In the book of Revelation, the State is God's ultimate enemy, busy exterminating the people of God. So John's vision sees the state replaced by a heavenly one. Christians have used the images in Revelation *in extremis*, when all hope for a reformed earthly city has disappeared. (For these four positions see Rogerson & Vincent, 2009: 99-101). So, we create

- Alternative Politics

In terms of present-day Christian urban communities wishing to follow a model based primarily on juggling with 1 and 2, but recognising areas within which 3 is necessary, this means we have a *political analysis of the biblical passage*. Here, we move into analysis of the *politics*, the strategy, the historical purpose, that the passage indicates. This is the view *out from* the reality. We want to know what predictable or plannable, political and organizational strategies are indicated (Vincent, 2005: 34).

Of course, not every one of the Gospel elements takes place in any one situational project or happening. But if some at least of the elements are not present, then something decisive is missing. At the end of a UTU Institute on Bible and Practice, I concluded:

We recreate the Gospel in our own time by repeating bits of the actions of the Gospels in our own contexts. We need the variety of Gospel stories to discover stories we are being called upon to re-enact, but also which contexts, problems, issues, people and communities these stories belong to (Vincent, in Rowland & Vincent, eds., 2001: 108).

So, our search for God's Project and Gospel Politics today leads us to search in the city, with questions like:

1. *Situation Analysis. Where* is this story at home? *What contexts* are like it? Who today feels especially at home in this biblical situation?

2. *Practice Analysis. With what* is this story at home? *What practice* is like it? Who today has practice or happenings like these scriptural ones?

3. *Endogenous Analysis. With whom* is this story at home? *What people* are like it? Who today has similar 'fire within' to the people in the biblical actions?

4. *Political Analysis. What movement* is this story like? *What policies* does it empower? What movement today would be coherent with the biblical strategy? (Vincent, 2005: 35)

13. CHRISTOLOGY

A Gospel-practice-based project following a Gospel methodology presses also at the level of the Imitation of Christ as key practitioner and paradigm.

This produces relevant but often contrary elements of Christology. From Mark's Gospel we may discern (Vincent, 1981: 22-35):

Jesus the Loner—without authentication, coming from nowhere.
Jesus the Deviant—against synagogue and temple, leading alternatives.
Jesus the Bondman—bound with the poor, bringing liberation.
Jesus the Juggler—weighing the eccentric with the communicable.
Jesus the Politician—pioneering alternatives within Judaism and Empire.
Jesus the Pied Piper—leading a movement of itinerant prophets.

To these I later added others (Vincent, 2004: 59-81):

Jesus the Alternative— creating new family and new agendas.
Jesus the Guru—being his Ashram's "Good Teacher".
Jesus the Master—sharing common life and destiny with disciples.
Jesus the Blasphemer—pretending to do what God does.
Jesus the Politician—exposing and opposing Temple and Rome.
Jesus the Counter-Politician—raising up new political community.
Jesus the Journey Downwards—birthing a new Divine Realm.

Shannahan has some intriguing new titles for a possible future "new cross-cultural symbolic urban Christology" (2010: 313)—Organic Intellectual, Stranger, Glocal, Story-teller, Brother, Insurgent, Plural, Refugee, Outsider/Insider, Unheard, God's Yes to the Oppressed. My current titles are Urban Guerilla, Divinity in Humanity, Secular Saint, Campaigner, Asylum Seeker, Project Manager, Street Pastor, Co-habitant, Bread-sharer, Homeless.

Beyond titles, a Christology of the Dynamics of Christ suggests sequential elements. Thus, in, *Into the City*, I describe eight aspects of urban mission experienced in SICEM as continuing eight key aspects of Jesus's ministry as recorded in the Gospels. I concluded that each aspect was necessary for the practice of urban mission:

1. *Incarnation.* We need to confirm ourselves in the areas of need. If we are not there, a few of us need to move there.

2. *Healing.* We need people on the ground who will express love and compassion in the face of obvious injustice and victimization.

3. *Parables.* We need people, preferably locals, who will take up the gut-level happenings of an area, and hold them up for others to see.

4. *Acted Parables.* We need visible examples, prophetic signs, acted parables, proleptic instances of what we want, set up for all to see.

5. *Disciple Group.* We need people really committed to each other, to the place, and to the disciplines necessary for significant acting.

6. *Crucifixion.* We need to be at the places where the oppression of the powers is really encountered and felt, so that we can be borne down by it, as others are borne down by it.

7. *Resurrection.* We need to be around when old things are raised up, when old things get started again, when the commitments crucified by the enemies are brought to life again.

8. *Parousia.* We need to be backyard visionaries, plucking from the future the things that all humanity seeks, and digging in bits of them in city backyards (Vincent, 1982: 136. Also in *The Cities*, 1997, 210).

In one sense, each level is built on the preceding one. We do not presume to tell parables or act parables until we have become part of the scene by incarnation, and dealt with a few glaring injustices by healing. We do not get to resurrection, except by the commitment of a group (disciple group) to action in face of the powers (acted parable), which is rewarded by the powers by refusal and rejection (crucifixion). And it is illegitimate to leap straight to strategies and proposals for the future (parousia) except on the basis of all the other levels, from incarnation to crucifixion and resurrection.

Thus, this connection between Christology and urban life manifests itself in very specific aspects of Christology and aspects of urban life being recalled in a sort of instinctive "matching". Simultaneously or by turns, the sequence describes aspects of Jesus's ministry in his own time, and aspects of the discipleship and mission of contemporary urban disciples. Inmundations of Gospel take place, and the secular Dynamics of Christ first revealed in the practice of the Jesus of the Gospel attains contemporaneity through the faithful practice of Jesus-embodiers and Jesus embodiments today.

14. DISCIPLESHIP

I had studied the Gospels in Basel with Oscar Cullmann and Bo Reicke, and Dogmatics with Karl Barth, and my 1960 thesis on Discipleship in Mark convinced me that you had to practice discipleship first, rather than initially teach it to others. So I arrived in Pitsmoor in 1970, convinced that one way to save biblical scholarship—and indeed Christianity—from its suburban and academic captivities would be by setting up an academic study unit based on practice in an area consonant with that in which Jesus, the originator of Christianity, chose to create his first community of followers, called "to be with him, and to be sent out to proclaim the message, and to have authority to cast out devils" (Mk. 3.14).

Six conclusions for practical discipleship came from my study of Discipleship in Mark (Vincent, 1975).

1. Discipleship is a literal "walking behind", in which the disciples follow the Way of the one to whom they are discipled. Discipleship is about physical movement, following a specific other person.

2. Discipleship implies a "leaving behind". Those called into discipleship remove themselves from other dominant controlling environments such as location, occupation, family, and dwelling. Jesus's incarnate "discipleship" was self-limiting (Vincent, 1982: 14-17). Ours is also.

3. Discipleship is an activity undertaken with fellow disciples, who form a *societas in cordibus* (Melanchthon), a committed group, who surround the leader and form a working community, with new locations, occupations, family and dwellings.

4. Discipleship includes elements of existence, lifestyle and practice which are embodiments or foretastes of a new style of existence, lifestyle and practice which Jesus calls the newly present New Realm of God here on earth (Mk.1.15).

5. Discipleship involves imitating the practice of the leader. Jesus became a friend of publicans and sinners (Mk. 2.15-17). Disciples carry out counter-cultural activity to embody this (Mk. 2.18-28), and involve in activity of healing and empowerment for the disadvantaged (Mk. 6.7-13; 9.14-29).

6. Discipleship confronts existing social, political and economic power holders with alternative practice, supporting and identifying with Jesus's rejection of Torah authorities (scribes and Pharisees), Temple controls (mediated forgiveness, etc.), Roman rule (tribute), and economic controls (absentee landlords). Disciples learn from Jesus the Counter-Politician (Vincent, 2004: 77-80).

Andrew Davey, thus outlines the continuing significance of the discipleship/Christology model:

The person and work of Christ has been essential to the vocations and writing of those engaged in urban mission and praxis. The radical perspectives found alongside communities of the poor, through faithful living and attentive reflection on the scriptures, have stimulated a hybrid, Christ-centred, urban missiology based around the themes of radical discipleship, incarnation and the kingdom of God (Davey, ed., 2000: 84).

These discipleship perspectives, it seems to me, are only capable of being studied through methods of experimental practice. The easiest way to discover whether experimental practice today would validate the perspectives is to find a location in which there might be some connections with the locations in rural-urban Galilee where the discipleship model was developed. Social, economic, cultural and political analyses of contemporary Britain, in 1970 or in 2013, suggest that the inner cities are a good place to start—and, indeed, have a strategic locational "hermeneutical advantage".

UTU's model is thus discipleship as following into a new place, involvement in a mission among the poor, rediscovering scriptural understanding through one's own experience, developing new forms of church, academy, mission and faith in the context, and engaging in political activity on the basis of the practice.

In the next chapter, we describe some of the "outworkings" of these Gospel Dynamics of Christ, seen as Urban Discipleship and Ministry stances and strategies in examples of practice by ourselves and colleagues, which suggest some further learnings in terms of the specifics of Community and Congregation today. In the final chapter, we indicate some engagements it has taken us into in the spheres of Community and Politics.

Chapter Three

OUTWORKINGS IN

DISCIPLESHIP AND MINISTRY

1. MINISTRY AS CHRISTO-CENTRIC VOCATION

This is the third book which I have written out of the experience of working in Sheffield. Grace and I and our family of three children arrived in 1970. The first volume *Into the City* tells the story of the foundation of the Urban Theology Unit, the Sheffield Inner City Ecumenical Mission, and the Sheffield Ashram House, in the early years of the 1970s. I picked up the model of Christology just given, and reflected on my ministerial experience, some thirty years ago (Vincent, 1982: 106-107):

Incarnation—digging in to an area
Healing—being used by people in need
Parables—telling messages already present
Acted Parables—acting out some new messages
Disciple Group—growing small committed groups
Crucifixion—being wounded by hostile forces
Resurrection—seeing small reversals of crucifixion
Parousia—identifying elements of ultimacy and value

In practice, my experience was that this basic Jesus/Gospel shaped Christological pattern has an "historical" side to it—so that you personally have to go through one stage before you can get into the next. But once you were expecting this "mind" of Christ to be at work in you (Phil. 2.5), then you found yourself being provoked, challenged, inspired and carried along by it. As I commented in those early years, "It was the Jesus of the streets. And the streets of Jesus were as full of the list of dramas and people and happenings and communities and enemies and heroes and heroines and betrayers and crucifiers—as were my streets." So the question to the Gospel became, "Which bits and which people, which scenes and which happenings, are coming alive around me now?" Jesus's "Project" had to start and continue with the dull specificities of particular people, places, meetings, events, communities and political realities. So do my Projects. So what can I learn from that?

Take the first stage—Incarnation. Most ministers initially come into an area from outside. They are "incomers", who have to assimilate themselves to an area and its people and issues. As "incomers", they especially seek in some way to share the life of the local people, to live alongside them, and then slowly to discover what ways they might work with those who are already there. In the second volume, *Hope from the City* (2000), I am still reflecting on Incarnation:

Indeed, I believe that the decisive gift of Christianity is this gift of incarnation—not just the gift of incarnation in Jesus, but the gift of constant incarnations. Each incarnation must begin from outside. It comes tentatively, fearfully to birth. It births itself in some part of the human *milieu*. It is subject to the disciplines, misunderstandings and oppressions of all around. It grows secretly, through silent years, growing till it is able furtively to appear. Then its 'messianic secret' suddenly comes out. An incarnation is a divine annunciation, a heavenly naming. And the Spirit demands a ludicrous claim that all people and all things and all communities will be changed—that the poor will get good news, the captives will get freedom, the broken will get wholeness (Luke 4.18) (Vincent, 2000: 127).

This ministry story as "incomer" and "incarnate" is very like the story of Jesus, which in turn is uncommonly like the story of many of my contemporaries in ministry, who become disciples of Jesus the Radical. They often come from middle class backgrounds but feel called to a ministry like Jesus's, which calling in turn lands them in some place of special need, where they seek to live out their discipleship and ministry along the same lines as Jesus. Like him, they make a "journey downwards" (Vincent, 2004: 81-84). Ian Wallis comments:

What we're after is nothing less than Jesus' take on being human, his characterization of personhood, the habitus of faith he embodied, that once identified, we may attempt to inhabit it also. This is an heuristic enterprise through which Jesus not only becomes visible, but is also reconstituted within the faith of his followers (Ian Wallis, in Vincent, ed., 2006: 194).

2. MINISTRY AS COMMUNITY WORK

The stage of Incarnation into the streets leads on to Healing, Parables and Acted Parables there. Today, this means that the minister becomes also a local community activist, a community organiser, and a community politician. Each of these he/she sees in Jesus. So Jesus is seen and used as a model for community ministry. He is, in our terms, a community worker.

Thus, the process and methodology visible in Jesus's ministry "come over" in the classic community developmental scheme in the mind and expectation of the contemporary community worker. This is the argument of *Radical Jesus* (Vincent, 2004: 9, passim). There are three stages visible in Mark's Gospel. Jesus's practice means that he:

1. Identifies with a specific sub-culture (11-24):
   Northerner
   Lower Middle Class
   Man of Roots
   Inner City Man

2. Proclaims new possibilities (27-41):
   Radical Happenings   1.14-20
   Radical Manifesto   1.1-14
   Liberates from Bondage   1.21-28
   Gives Power to the People 1.29-45

3. Practices New Community (41-56):
   Solidarity with the Poor 2.1-17
   Parties in Houses   2.18-27
   Partnership with Women   3.31-35
   Success to the Struggle   3.1-30
   Welcome to Foreigners   5.1-20

This is the content of "The Kingdom Movement" which disciples take out in Mission in Mark 6.

Of course, there have to be elements of "translation" from a first century Jesus ministry to a 21st century professional denominational ministry or community work practice. But some elements continue.

In a consultation with a group of ministers, we tried to set down some of the present day implications of this Jesus-style ministry (2004: 100):

Listening to the groaning and travailing of the city,
Sharing skills and experience and learning communally,
Learning with pioneers working alongside poor and disadvantaged people,
Provoking and supporting each other honestly, critically and creatively,
Helping people to face unpleasant realities and take risks,
Renewing ourselves and each other in places where life is draining,
Searching with others for new vocations and ways of being disciples,
Exploring new personal and corporate styles of Doing Theology,
Supporting people in struggling situations, small churches and alternative
                                                                communities,
Being grasped in fresh ways by Jesus and the Gospel,
Raiding the Christian storehouse to offer fresh tools and ingredients,
Existing by faith, in smallness and simplicity,
Encouraging the transformation of society by being irritants, models and
                                                                catalysts.

The tradition of ministry through community work is widespread today (cf. Ballard & Husselbee, 2008), and invites continuing theological reconstruction.

3. DISCIPLESHIP AS WALKING THE WORD

The same is true for Discipleship in the inner city.

In at least three strands, the way set out in the Gospels resonates with contemporary practice and understanding of Discipleship, of the Disciple

Group, and of the Imitation of Jesus. I give examples from my own experience.

1. *Discipleship.* I have personally found myself drawn deeper into the Gospel of Mark as an urban disciple, following the beginnings of "An Urban Hearing for the Gospel" (in Rowland and Vincent, eds., 1997: 105-116), and then in a series of articles in the *Expository Times* on "Gospel Practice Criticism", "Gospel Practice Today", and "The Practice of Disciples" (reprinted in Vincent, 2005: 2-27). A contribution by John Riches on "John Vincent's 'Outworkings'" led to "Outworkings: Next Steps" (Vincent, 2005: 28-36). In all these, the contemporary experiences of discipleship as practiced by inner city disciples have provided the "outworking" in a way that seems natural and provocative (Vincent, 2007; Hooker & Vincent, 2010).

2. *Disciple Group.* The five stories of the disciples in Mark 2 feature healing as forgiveness (1–12), eating with tax-collectors (13-17), feasting not fasting (18–22), breaking Sabbath (23–28), and synagogue healing (3.1-6) and suggest coherent practice in the small street-corner inner city shop-front church at Grimesthorpe (Vincent, 2007a). Similarly, aspects of the calling and tasking of the Twelve disciples in Mark 3 provoke responses and practice in the life of a post-denominational "fresh expression" inner city para-church in the Burngreave Ashram (Vincent, 2008). I have continued this with work on the Parables in Mark 4 as a set of models whereby disciple groups identify secular happenings around them as indications of Realm-of-God significance (Vincent 2011c). The Journey to Gerasa in Mark 5 appears as a story for disciple groups dealing with other faiths (Vincent, 2013).

3. *Imitation.* There are also ways in which, once one has established a location which seems to "cohere with", or "be comfortable with", or "make connections with" (Rogerson & Vincent, 2009: 103-105), a Gospel location, then one finds that one urban Gospel thing follows another urban Gospel thing. Thus, the walk or Way of Jesus and his followers along roads and lanes of rural-urban Galilee (2009, 56-59) provokes imaginative rehearsal of similar walking in similar situations facing similar issues with similar pieces of "obedience". So the Way of Jesus in Mark's urban-rural Galilee provokes similar perceptions and namings, and similar discipleship ventures and schemes, in contemporary urban Sheffield (Hooker & Vincent, 2010: 33-67). This is surely an "Imitation of Jesus",

but an imitation not of spirituality, personality, "good traits" or even intentionality. Rather, it is an imitation of Jesus in his deeds, his practice, his relationships, his schemes, his projects, his self-precipitations, his openness to violence, his *handlings* of things.

In 2008, twenty members of Ashram Community spent a week at Iona Abbey. We studied Discipleship in Mark as part of a search for "Christian Community in the 21st Century". Five groups looked at key passages:

1.14- 20	The Call
2.13-17	The Common Mission
3.13-19	The Community
6.8-11	The Common Disciplines
10.28-31	The Personal Consequences

With each passage, we asked ourselves four questions: 1. What are the *characteristics* of discipleship here? 2. What *process* is taking place in discipleship? 3. What *degrees* of discipleship are evident? 4. What exactly is *shared* here? (Hooker & Vincent, 2010: 43-44, 50, 57-61)

So discipleship as walking the word involves critical engagement between disciple group and biblical text leading to practical imitation of Jesus in today's world.

4. DEVELOPING A GOSPEL PROJECT

The process of Gospel Contextual Discernment always leads to some kind of Practice or Action, often a Project (Chapter Two, Section 11).

Working with local groups or congregations, a simpler model is needed which allows members to do work from their perceived experience, plus Gospel Study, towards human group development and utilisation of local resources.

A model for this is:

DYNAMICS OF A GOSPEL PROJECT

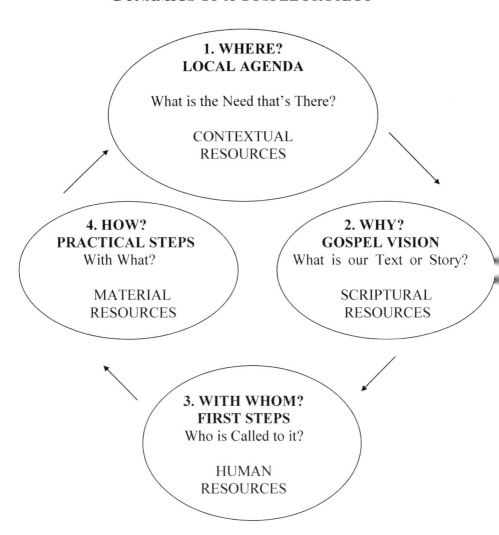

This simple working model was employed in the early days of our group at Burngreave Ashram in 2001–2002. It gave us a variety of inviting openings and possibilities, many of which came to fruition in various ways in the years that followed:

A GOSPEL PROJECT

1. Local Agenda	2. Gospel Vision	3. & 4. First Steps & Action
Poor health Anti-ecological lifestyle Early mortality rates	SEEDS GROWING (Mk. 4.26-29) Seeds of alternative, sustainable life	NEW ROOTS CAFE Experiment with various sales and uses
Inter-racial conflict Alienation Fear	DISCIPLE COMMUNITY (Mk. 1.16-23, 3.14) Two or three—Follow me	COMMUNITY FLATS Homeless and Asylum Seekers Residential Accommodation
Lack of Community Little training Lack of meeting space	OPEN HOUSE (Acts 2.43-47) Food & Fellowship Political forum	DANCE STUDIO Start Café Church Gathering in houses
Deprivation Multiple needs Lack of ministry	JESUS'S HOUSE (Mk. 2.1-12) Personal ministries	OFFICES Bases for local workers Contact points
Lack of places for local initiatives	POTTER'S HOUSE (Jer. 18.2, Acts 4.32-27)	CELLAR Make space available

5. URBAN GOSPEL MINISTRY PROJECTS

This "working together" of context and text leading to practice has been the method that has produced many striking results in terms of both project and theological discernment. I give a few examples from UTU dissertations by urban pastors, each of them focussed on expanding a Christian community's service to its neighbourhood.

1. Jane Grinonneau led the Baptist Church in Northfield, Birmingham, into exposure to the lives of the deprived children on the Allens Cross Estate. A study of Jesus's ministry with children reveals that childlikeness, and an attitude of receiving children, are keys to Realm of God practice.

Key Gospel elements are the boy (*paidarion*) of John 6.9, and above all, Jesus's statements of Mark 10.14-15: "Let the children come to me, do not prevent them, because the Realm of God belongs to such as these. I assure you that whoever does not receive the Realm of God as a child will never enter it".

The church then studied aspects of being a child which might assist their search for childlikeness. Among such "entry criteria" were found to be absence of learning, status, wealth and power, and absence of possessions.

> The child receives with empty hands. Jesus calls his disciples to give up what they had held and valued, because in their losing everything they would gain so much more (Mk. 10.21, 29-30).

The conclusion was to set up an open after-school club for local children.

> As the church received children onto its premises, it discovered through them the absence of childlikeness in its own name. The children acted as agents of liberation to the church, ultimately releasing the church from its un-childlike nature into a more faithful expression of childlikeness to which Jesus calls us (Grinonneau, 2000: 104-110).

The dissertation then concludes with outlines of some implications for churches based on the childlikeness model.

2. Paul Shackerley as Vice-Dean of Sheffield Cathedral worked with city, congregation and trustees to develop a highly significant Centre for the Homeless.

> Every morning, the Archer Project is faced with a frenetic hustle of homeless people. They pressure the staff to respond to their immediate demands. They express a sense of urgency to be fed, to see the nurse or dentist, demanding food parcels, shower, launder their clothes, and clamour to telephone the Council Housing Department. Then they return to the streets to sell the Big Issue, or move on somewhere for no reason other than sleeping in a skip or wandering the city streets. Others sit in the lounge, reading the daily paper, listening to music and accessing the internet, wait for their Giro to arrive by post, watching television, or wait for the nurse, shower, or breakfast. This is a place of loitering and

impatient waiting for a service. Initially, there is anger, chaos and urgency. At least, until they realise there is time and safety. They do not have to behave this way. It is a safe place of hospitality, where they can converse without anger and urgency with their neighbour and with the staff (Shackerley, 2007: 261).

Crucial in his discovery of "the practice of hospitality on the margins" was the congregation's discovery of the significance of the Feeding of the Five Thousand in John 6.1-13 and Luke 9.10-17. Shackerley writes (259):

In John's account of the feeding of the five thousand, the Disciples were encouraged to feed the crowd when a diminutive boy appeared from the crowd as a giver (John 6:10). This was a crucial action by a diminutive person, who came forward with little food (John 6:8-9). Everything appears without prospect about the person. Yet, not only was he diminutive in social status and class, but he was doubly diminutive because he was a slave and a child. His contribution of barley loaves indicates his offering was poor quality, yet the boy was ahead of the action, offering his contribution. His role was decisive for the continuation of giving, blessing, and thanksgiving for others. The crowd was treated with dignity as gift-givers. That is how guests and givers are to be experienced. As an authentic rendezvous with the stranger, immigrant, and homeless, the Church should not forget what the marginalised potentially offer the givers of hospitality.

Shackerley observes in his own experience how "from their poverty and exclusion, the poor can offer insights, powerful narratives, and practical support to others. This story illustrates how Christ's disciples feed the crowd not by providing out of their own spiritual and material resources, but through turning to the unexpected places where the guest is a giver, no matter what small amount is given" (259).

3. Paul Walker, Minister of Highgate Baptist Church in Birmingham (1996: 96-112) sees an "Urban Mysticism" developing through the "solidarity, friendship and relationships" which he and the church have as they "loiter with intent", and visit and talk with people in Magnolia House (elderly mentally infirm), the "Shakti" Day Centre, the community centre

at Matthew Boulton College, and the Ale Stake public house, local schools, centres and shops.

The church had hit on the Parable of the Sheep and the Goats in Matthew 25.31-46 as its provoking scriptural partner:

> We believe that it is only when both care for others and political action are grounded in mystical values similar to those found in the Story of the Sheep and the Goats and in the Gospel of which it is a part, a mystical vision born of our urban reality, that human life will be transformed. As our eyes are opened to see the City as 'Thou', the poor person as 'the Christ', this space as 'Holy Ground' and this moment as the 'Eternal now', we see differently, but more truly. Such 'seeing' changes us and the world about us. Such an urban mysticism overturns the current values of capitalist culture and empowers the individual person and the community to live the new life now—in miniature and in anticipation (215).

A polity of vulnerability and partnership with strangers emerges.

6. URBAN GOSPEL DISCIPLESHIP PROJECTS

In some of our projects and dissertations on them, the focus remains upon ministry, but deals primarily with areas of personal discovery and discipleship. Three examples follow.

1. Stuart Ware reflects deeply on an experience of imprisonment, and on work with prisoners and ex-prisoners. He sees the scriptural paradigm of God in Jesus as "the non-violent God who was incarcerated and executed, and in so doing, became our liberator."

He writes: "God, through Jesus, identifies with us in our suffering and offers hope in the midst of our incarcerations. For the early Christians, the incarcerated and executed Jesus created a sense of loss and confusion. Seeking for explanations of the crucifixion of Jesus, they turned to the sacrificial imagery of the Hebrew Scriptures. I find this perfectly understandable, bearing in mind their Jewish cultural heritage and influential 'Rabbinic understandings of sacrifice'."

But then goes on: "A theology of the incarcerated challenges the focus on the vicarious suffering of Jesus that has been emphasised by the institutional Church to the detriment of an inclusive community of reconciliation. Therefore, our opposition to retributive concepts of punishment that permeate our modern penal system has a theological basis: religion relies on violence to retain its power and authority, especially when allied with the State. Jesus challenged this violence and was silenced. Violence removes all vestiges of hope" (Ware, 2006: 163).

Ware concludes (164) that "there is the risk that 'dangerous memories' become so introspective and self-protective, dwelling only on the negative experiences of the past to dictate and justify the present." What is needed is "a theology in which the objects become the subject, moving from an excluded community to the Community of the Reconciled … embodying a theology of the incarcerated" based also on "belief in a future hope when all appears to be lost."

2. Debbie Herring carried out two years of research with a Cyberspace Usenet community (usenetgroup.uk.religion.christian), concerning how they see their "community", and how they see its theology. Their theologising is "in", "of" and "for" the context, and the nearest thing to it emerges as the Trinitarian *perichoresis* theology of the eastern Church.

In this context, a *"perichoretic"* community appears, characterised by *koinonia*, human mutual indwelling, and a "dancing together", a *perichoresis*. Herring writes: "The idea of mutually indwelling relationships between self and others, dancing around chaotically but remaining in community, has for 1700 years been used by Christians to describe the inner life of God. Community in cyberspace reflects this profoundest concept of community that Christianity has discovered. At the risk of enraging those systematic theologians who prefer to reserve all religious language for their own use, it is entirely appropriate to liberate the term *perichoresis* into secular language for the use of those exploring new forms of community, acknowledging that Christian theology has done us all a service by preserving it as a model of community which resonates so richly with contemporary experience." (Herring, 2005: 217-218).

Contemporary cyberspace thus makes possible a new form of "church" as a mutually reactive and creative community.

3. Keith S. Lackenby works with two country chapels, and they discover that their "tabernacles", their "tents of meeting", need to continue in a new place, nearer the centre of the town.

The new church is designed to be "an open space", from which the footpath and traffic outside are very visible, which has accessible and multi-purpose rooms—but yet has all the "secret" treasures of the two chapels' remembered past.

Lackenby writes: "The tension between the elaborate Tabernacle of the 'P' Tradition and the more simple Tent of Meeting of the 'E' Tradition touched a raw nerve. We too had our idealised models of the Church and her mission, strict ideas about sacred space, hung with the chintz curtains of the illusions we cherish. The ancient texts shattered these illusions. They served to interpret the theological direction in which we were beginning to move. In the event, this was a truly double edged hermeneutic, for as the scriptures interpreted the life of the church, the scriptures were at the same time interpreted in the light of the questions and concerns of the local church. This is the way Scripture is handled by liberation theologians, who are never concerned to interpret Scripture or the traditions of the church in the abstract; rather they are anxious to bring the issues that arise out of their social and political situation to bear on the text" (Lackenby, 1990: 100-101).

In this way, "the lives of women and men are enmeshed in the story of salvation history to the extent that their lives are part of the continuing purpose of God. Christian people will always find themselves in a dialogue with the Biblical texts in such a way that they pose their own questions to the texts and formulate their answers on the basis of what they read" (101).

Lackenby concludes (101) that we have come "back to the oral tradition when the saving acts of God were recalled, and reshaped in the light of the present circumstance in which the people of God were seeking to live out their faith. Perhaps theology and praxis are not modern principles of theological engagement, but reach back to the Priest's reworking of the ancient traditions during the Exilic period, continued by the first Christians who told and retold the stories of Jesus in the kerygma, and are carried on wherever the Word is heard and applied in faith and practice.

Perhaps Scripture and tradition have always been shaped by audience understanding."

7. OUTWORKINGS IN CONGREGATIONS

The relation of our work to the growing area of studies of congregations/churches remains open. One implication of our work is that the approaches of anthropology, sociology and organisational studies utilised in congregational studies, as in Cameron, Richter, Davies & Ward (2005) could and should be applied to the study of practice. Equally, the variety and character of "practice" in particular church settings needs study and categorisation. Also, at present, the element of theology in congregational studies remains somewhat undeveloped, un-nuanced and theoretical. Our scriptural/theological model now needs to be added to the spectrum of perspectives.

Our experience is that the method of correlation between Gospel Models and Ministry Practice occurs also in many more undeveloped ways in inner city and housing estate ministry. I give three instances from *Faithfulness in the City* (2003).

1. The parable of the Kingdom as being like yeast (Mt. 13.33) means that a small congregation on a deprived estate concludes that: "Even a small number in comparison to the masses can have a significant effect. To have an effect, two things are essential. We must mix into the local culture, as the yeast mixes into the dough, and we must live out our Christianity in that context, just as the yeast dispenses its own life on the surrounding dough" (Derek Purnell, p. 70).

2. A housing estate group of untrained helpers stumble into their project of Frankie's, a youth café, and make endless mistakes, but find unexpected blessings. Then, looking back, "they see how their practice has in fact embodied pieces of the Gospel story of Jesus" (Peter Howard, p. 74).

3. Similarly, a city congregation finds that certain Gospel slogans and vignettes become springboards for action, and develop mission statements and methods of working. "Seven elements from Jesus's practice" provoke action (Geoff Curtiss, p. 75).

Sometimes, congregations begin with the Jesus story, and find or create a happening of their own that reflects it. At other times, they find that what has been happening, either by plan or by circumstance, reflects back into a Jesus story. So the question is, "What Jesus story have we seen?" But also another question, "What have we seen that points to a Jesus story?" So, at a Half Day, branches of SICEM shared their stories in this way (Vincent, 2000: 109-116) and wrote (114):

> The stories of Jesus are in the background. The Jesus actions function as a repeated model or dynamic. We don't have to produce texts all the time, but it is a determining thing, telling us what is important, and giving us the instincts and the imagination to do certain things, and not to do other things.

They then added that it's not just Story Telling. It's also "Story-Acting". "We do the story as a way of telling it. It's a re-enacting of the story of Jesus in our stories. We do not have to tell a good story, we are acting a good story. When we do talk, it's simply to describe what has been happening. We have moved from being story-hearers to being story-actors and thus story-creators" (114).

Such story-acting is precisely the "witness" of disciples, the continuing of the string of Gospel *martyria*, the "faithfulness" both as "the phenomenon of being 'full of faith'" as shown in practice, and also as "the long time survival and authenticity of individuals at the sharp edges of society" (*Faithfulness in the City*, 2003: 305).

In a talk on "Gospel Values in Inner City Churches", my former SICEM colleague Duncan Wilson listed the following:

> Where Christ and his people are,
> they make clear that everyone is a child of God;
>> that those not within the church are not necessarily far from the Kingdom of God;
> they lay a table where all are welcome, where strangers find a home;
> they recognize that everyone has an offering to bring;
> they find faith where no one else looks for it;
> they notice people whom others ignore or diminish;
> they celebrate the 'greatness of the small';

they give space for everyone to fail, to learn, to grow;
they make mercy and generosity servants of renewal;
they never force an entry into other people's lives;
they warn against making rules more important than relationships;
they show that love finds joy in being spent;
    that being broken or vulnerable also reveals God's presence;
they expect change to be possible for everyone;
they patiently wait to find each person's 'touching place';
    and promise that, wherever Christ is,
    the blind do recover their sight,
    the lame do walk,
    the deaf do hear,
    the dumb do speak,
    the dying are brought to life
    and the poor do hear good news.
(in Rowland & Vincent, eds, 1997: 104)

Such a list as that of Duncan Wilson just quoted gives a good feel for the way in which congregations regard Projects, and subjectively reflect theologically on Projects.

8. THE GOSPEL COMMUNITY

Urban Theologising is often done by individuals with a sense of call, and some kind of position or place within a context. But the individual is always part of some sort of community. And if they do not have a community at the outset, they find or create one, either already related to their vocational theologising, or one that might be won over to it, or even come into existence around it.

Thus, in Situation Analysis, the student/practitioner initially conducts a detailed examination and research around all the people, institutions, issues and experiences of the neighbourhood or area, but then conducts an equally rigorous examination of the Christian Community of which they are a part (Duffield, 2011).

Over the 40 years since UTU's first Urban Ministry Course in 1971, the people in this position have varied considerably. In my own locality, in

1971 there were five Christian churches, mainly of traditional denominations. Today, in 2010, there are eleven, with fewer traditional denominations, now joined by 18 non-Christian faith groups, including seven Mosques. So that a community intentionally committed to a Christian theological enterprise is rather different today. Within inner city Christian communities and churches, the question of "What is a Gospel Community?" continues to exercise us. The question, "What is a Church?" was raised when SICEM first welcomed the Ashram Community House as a constituent member in 1972 (Vincent, 1982: 39-41). It then produced a lively debate about "The Marks of a Church".

Recently I have been working with three north-west candidates in the 2008 cohort for the MPhil/PhD in Contextual, Urban and Liberation Theologies. One is working on "Fresh Expressions" in Liverpool Methodist churches, another on "Urban Walking" on a Liverpool housing estate, another on "Ministry With" in inner city South Manchester. Our seminar on "Theological Practice", quickly got on to the question of "Who does Theological Practice?"—i.e. what or which group is, in fact, the community engaged in the Pastoral Cycle, the Hermeneutical Cycle, the experimental practice, the discernment of mission, the embodiment in faith of Jesus-consistent devotion and activity?

The question, "What is the Church?" becomes very specifically a question about visible practices. If the Marks of the Church have anything to do with the Marks of Jesus Practice, then it is these which are embodied in a contemporary "Holy, Catholic and Apostolic" community. Existing local churches and congregations, of course, can be part of this, or the springboard for it.

My own most recent reflections on this conundrum were provoked by the experience of writing the history of the Ashram Community. As a result, I concluded that there were several vital "threads" that ran through all the bits and pieces of that story. They have, in fact, historically been features of the activity of Christian churches and communities down the ages (Vincent, 2009):

1. Calling. What is our special calling or charism?
2. Discovering. Where do we find our dominant biblical and theological inspirations?

3. Gathering. How do we get together to pursue our corporate life?
4. Home Sharing. What are the particular manifestations of our ethos in fellowship life?
5. Project Sharing. How in practical schemes do we get on to the streets?
6. Risking Ourselves. What internal disciplines do we establish to keep it all together?

I took a similar set of questions to ten other contemporary British Intentional Communities. It is striking to observe how these essentially Gospel-style aspects of Christian Community are being lived out in the stories of Anabaptist/Mennonite, Hillfields, Iona, L'Arche, Lee Abbey, Northumbria, Othona, Pilsdon, SCK and the Well Communities today (Vincent, ed., 2011b).

9. WORSHIP AND SPIRITUALITY

A recent book of essays shows how the characteristic worship of inner city churches derives from the realities of the people who are there and the effects of the context around them (Stratford, ed., 2006). Ann Morisy and Ann Jeffries comment:

It is more appropriate to think in terms of participants rather than 'worshippers'. Worship is hard to achieve when the head is burning as to whether one has faith or whether one really believes in the orthodoxies of a religion (in Stratford, ed., 2006, 72).

Morisy and Jeffries give a list of "distinguishing features" for participant-led urban worship, which

- is grounded in people's experience, concerns or dilemmas.
- acknowledges, articulates and respects strong feelings.
- promotes a sense of solidarity with and empathy for others.
- suggests new perspectives, enabling understanding and awareness.
- provides opportunities for reflection in light of Scripture.
- develops a sense of the alongsideness of God.
- introduces basic religious symbols and concepts that can be pondered over time and drawn on.

- stimulates hope, confidence and the will for renewal and/or action (2006: 62).

Other factors influence the actual specifics of inner city worship. My own chapter in Tim Stratford's book (2006: 25-40) describes three urban worship occasions where the worship:

- is in small culturally distinctive, internally coherent groupings.
- reflects the discipleship and projects of the group.
- is a continuing process of trial and error, using gifts available.
- is supportive of mission and vocation, not an end in itself.
- often has a strong post-denominational character (28-29).

The theology of worship deriving from all this is itself significant:

> The liturgy is not the first thing: the Christian 'movement', the appearing of signs of the Kingdom of God, is the first thing. The liturgy is needed as a place to sink back into, away from the real presence of God in the secular and in the congregation and neighbourhood political and healing practice. The liturgy is not the driving force, but the underground discipline and structure for the community's vocation and mission (29).

Spirituality in urban Christianity has always had a rather mundane ethos. The city as a whole is obviously the scene of all kinds of spirituality (Walker, ed., 2005). But the housing estate has produced survival rather than esotericism, and the inner city congregation is often held together by conservative piety and conventional prayer routines. Yet the spirituality is singular, "known in the vivacity, warmth and mutual support of many poor urban communities" (Gorringe, 2002: 161). "Prophets get low" and "burn out" follows (Green, 2003: 135-137), so that a very practical spirituality is needed, which includes getting "outside the box", resting on colleagues, and acknowledging one's limitations (2003: 137-141). In the end, it is a kind of "Secular Jesus Spirituality", a "Spirituality of Jesus-centred Liberation and Wholeness", a new style *Liberation Spirituality* (Rowland & Vincent, eds., 1999: 102). It is a Spirituality of Mutuality, Weakness, Perseverance, Vulnerability, Rootedness, Loving Oneself, and Knowing When to Let Go, as Jan Royan says (61-67).

There are few "fruits" to pluck and take. Yet Laurie Green (in Davey, ed., 2010: 108) asks "Where would I go to make spiritual retreat? The countryside? Or, should I turn my face to the city or the housing estate and see the tears of Jesus in the face of the old woman in the market?"

Today we occasionally provide Inner City Retreats here in Burngreave and we have developed Sheffield Ashram Weeks, when we invite people from suburbs and countryside to a programme of Work, Pray, Study and Play, living and working with our local Community Houses and Members. This proves to be a very practical, secular and revelatory way of "re-enchanting the city with the seeds of the sacred" and delving "the spiritual potential of urban spaces" (Walker & Kennedy, 2011). We discover a spirituality not of "thin places" where (they told us on Iona) the transcendent is near the surface, but of "thick places" where the transcendent is deep down.

10. HYMN SINGING

John Atherton talks of a view of Christianity to "refute the neo-Barthianism of Hauerwas and the post-modern Christendom of Milbank" to "keep our feet firmly on the ground of church as hymn singing and meals on wheels" (Atherton, 2011, 131), and goes on:

> Being church is about an identity which includes dialogue and outreach through worship and service as its distinctive heart. Making connections with other 'convictions and aspirations' to address common problematics becomes an intimate part of ministry and mission (132).

That is certainly our concern at UTU. The prime question is therefore always to go back to the distinctive "convictions and aspirations" that a Christian group would be coming with.

"Hymns and meals on wheels" are exactly where we start at UTU. That is, we start with how urban Christians customarily express their faith. On the one hand, this means appropriate grass-roots verbal expression of a relevant faith. On the other hand, it means coherent practice, in terms of relevant action.

Urban Christians inherit the long tradition of song in working class communities. My own communion, Methodism, was "born in song"—at least that has been a truism stated throughout my lifetime. So in 1988, I appealed for some hymns "from the bottom". A hundred were submitted, from which we selected 31 and published them as *Hymns of the City* (Vincent, ed., 1989/1998). Three are from John Bell and Graham Maule, two from Fred Kaan and one from Fred Pratt Green. Four are resurrected from the old *Methodist Hymn Book* of 1933, excluded from its replacement *Hymns and Psalms* (1983)—"And did those feet", "Once to every man and nation", "These things shall be", and Ebenezer Elliott's "When wilt thou save the people?" (also in the musical *Godspell*). And we rediscovered a Charles Wesley:

My dearly beloved, your calling you see;
In Jesus approved, no goodness have we,
No riches or merit, no wisdom or might,
But all things inherit, through Jesus's right.
(Charles Wesley, No.16)

The other 20 hymns came from ministers and people in urban churches. I noted three characteristics.

First, the hymns are about people's real experience, and not the endless "Praise" for no particular reason, as seems to be the custom of the affluent churches. Secondly, the hymns are mainly about Jesus Christ. His starkness, his angularity, his provocation, his unexpectedness, as well as his poverty and his mission alongside the poor, comprise a style suited to urban survivors and prophets. There is little place for abstract concepts or general humanist goodwill. Thirdly, the hymns use largely old, well established tunes, rather than requiring new ones. They can be sung unaccompanied, which suits many urban congregations, where musicians are unavailable (Vincent, ed., 1989/1998: 3).

The assumption in the hymns is often that in some mysterious way, the stories of Jesus in the Gospels are now continuing on the streets of the city. The result is therefore a liturgical methodology based upon the identification of situation-specific Gospel actions by Jesus in the Gospels with similar situation-specific actions seen in characteristics and/or people today.

11. JESUS RECONSTRUCTION IN HYMNS

The imaginative reconstruction begins with a placement of Gospel incarnation in the contemporary city:

On the streets of every city, let the love of Christ be seen.
And then let us gladly follow, to the places he has been.
We will mount the steps of tower blocks, we ride the busy train,
In the frailty of his body, he will walk the streets again.
(David Hill, No.20)

Characteristics of Jesus's ministry in Galilee with people are reflected in similar characteristics of contemporary cities and their people:

Yours the city, yours the city,
With no place to lay your head.
Yours the courage, yours the pity,
Yours the life among the dead.
Yours the poor, and yours the beaten,
Struggling to reclaim their rights.
Yours the victimised we threaten,
Seeking allies for their fights.
(John Vincent, No.31)

The characteristic responses of Jesus to people in need are seen today in similar responses by his disciples in the city. Specifically, Gospel commensality continues in contemporary "soup kitchens":

In our city life is caring,
Thanks be to God;
Caring shown through human sharing,
Thanks be to God:
Caring which will heal our schisms,
Lift suspicion, cross divisions;
For these gifts of love's provisions
Thanks be to God.
(Clive Scott, No.10)

The soup kitchens, theologically, are part of the messianic banquet which Jesus shares with the poor and excluded (Lk. 14.15–21):

> With the people of the city, let the love of Christ be shared.
> Let us give the invitation to the feast he has prepared.
> For his table it is open, let our hearts be open too.
> In the loving of his body, he our cities will renew.
> (David Hill, No.20)

Alongside the soup kitchen, the hymns give rise to the wider vision which has "intimations" of a renewed city everywhere, already present in part in the Christian community's singing:

> In our city life is singing,
> Thanks be to God;
> Singing out a new beginning,
> Thanks be to God.
> Singing in anticipation,
> Sharing in God's new creation;
> Sing in eager expectation—
> Thanks be to God.
> (Clive Scott, No.10)

The good news of Jesus that the Realm of God is now present on earth is continued in practices by contemporary followers which continue the elements of the first embodiment:

> Yours the movement for empowering,
> Yours the kingdom, sure and meek,
> Yours the banquet for our flowering,
> Yours the shalom cities seek.
> Ours your faithful love upholding,
> Ours your grace outpassing fears,
> Ours the mystery unfolding—
> Christ who wipes away all tears!
> (John Vincent, No.31)

Not least, the "commensality" of Jesus and the Jesus community extends to include people on the frontiers, especially those of different ethnic groups. This recalls the "I have a dream" speech of Martin Luther King:

We have a dream, we have a dream
This nation's folk both black and white,
Will sit together at the Feast
As sons and daughters in God's sight.

We have a dream, we have a dream
That North and South, both rich and poor,
Will hear the message of the Christ
That all must share God's harvest store.
(Martin Eggleton, No.27)

The hymns constantly "firm up" contemporary disciples who see themselves as intentional followers of the practice of Jesus. Probably the most frequently sung of all hymns in urban churches is "Will you come and follow me?":

Will you come and follow me
If I but call your name?
Will you go where you don't know
And never be the same?
Will you let my love be shown,
Will you let my name be known,
Will you let my life be grown
In you and you in me?
(John Bell & Graham Maule, No.30)

This inner city and housing estate following of Jesus becomes manifest in specific ways, as it did for Jesus:

Will you let the blinded see
If I but call your name?
Will you set the prisoners free
And never be the same?
Will you kiss the leper clean,
And do such as this unseen,

And admit to what I mean,
In you and you in me?
(John Bell & Graham Maule, No.30)

And, of course, there is an element of "Make Affluence History":

Come, you for whom life is secure;
Step out on the road of the cross.
Share all that you have with the poor,
Set free from your terror of loss.
See, hear, with new eyes, with new ears;
Make practical loving your aim;
Takes risks (a companion is near)
With Jesus, a new world to gain.
(David Rice, No.32)

As with all theology, there are the lineaments of these earthly practices of ministry with places and people of need, and the building up of a Christ-mysticism of self-denying/self-fulfilling discipleship among followers. But these vital elements are set within a cosmological "divine plan" which finds its embodiment within them. The day of God's new world on this planet marks the end of all false hopes of other worlds, however much they seem bolstered up by contemporary values and systems:

The structured power
Of privilege and greed
Has had its hour
With this incarnate deed.
In grounded love
At Bethlehem's poor home
The people's friend,
The people's friend has come!

The wealth-wrapped few
Compassionless and cold,
Have had their due,
As all the prophets told.
The star now shines
On Bethlehem's poor home;

The people's friend,
The people's friend has come!
(Clive Scott, No.24)

Inner city hymns and theology are mainly "constructive". Kathy Galloway quotes hymns that voice pain, ridicule established power, and are gestures of defiance (2006: 14-24). Ours tend to emphasise a Christ-model response of love, ministry and companionship. That is, people usually prefer to sing about "what is going for them", rather than about what their enemies are up to.

12. MEALS ON WHEELS

When "Meals on Wheels" is joined with Hymns, the two gut-elements of the urban church come into place. John Atherton provides a theoretical justification for this. First, it is "multi-layered"—the layers of the diverse local community, the layer of "flows" from outside and across, the layer of the "wild card" of post-modern plurality, of "pick and mix", of networking and special interests. Second, it is "bottom-up", with local community groups, self-empowered, rejecting top-down strategies. Third, it is "in and for the community", drawing deeply from the internal dynamics of church life, relating intimately to other local communities and bodies, being a partner in local regeneration (Atherton, 2003: 132-136).

Our experience at UTU is that, just as the Hymns need to be taken more seriously, so does the "Meals on Wheels". It is a commonplace of contemporary writing on practical theology that practice is the way that faith is expressed, that "the practice is all".

The social and community projects and practice of urban churches and congregations has been covered in a number of recent reports, and need not be repeated here. Our particular aim has been to illustrate scriptural and/or theological content or intent, an element often not named, though it was and is frequently a crucial element in the project's formation. That said, readers may get some feel for the varieties of contemporary social and community ministries from recent publications, notably *Faithful Cities* (2006): 70-82, *Moral, But No Compass* (2008): 109-130, and *Churches in Action* (2009).

As *Faithful Cities* says: "The stories, scriptures, songs, prayers, rituals and teachings that form the everyday life of religious faith (the "habits of the heart") are not some anthropological curiosity. They are the source of the values which prompt action on behalf of those who are marginalised. The practices of faith and the actions of the faithful on behalf of their neighbour cannot be separated" (8.22).

Christians bring to the table their own particular "concerns" or "prejudices"—like (Garner, 2004: 85-112) Partnership, A Social God, Dialogue, and Christian Identity. How these work out both via scripture and in actual practice is always the test. In 2013 it is often Free Meals.

In 1981, when asked for a title for Methodism's Inner City Projects Campaign, I suggested that we avoided "Mission to", or "for", or "of the poor", and go for the more modest but evocative "Mission Alongside the Poor". It worked well for nearly two decades of imaginative neighbourhood ministry projects.

As with the hymns, the urban church has much specific "fruits" to show, regarding its practice—its faith-containing practice.

Burngreave Ashram is a local example. Its story is not untypical of many inner city "Missions Alongside the Poor" or "Fresh Expressions".

13. AT BURNGREAVE ASHRAM

The methodology of this chapter derives partly from social-science style Situation Analysis, partly from Gospel-style Theological Analysis, and partly from endless experimentation "in faith" in actual Practice. I here describe what this has meant in personal terms in a ministry I am involved with at present.

The Ashram Community Trust has a history of setting up inner city community houses and projects (Vincent, 2009: 63-98). In 2000, they bought the rambling shops, flats, community rooms and workshops of 80-86 Spital Hill and 25-31 Hallcar Street. It was a large set of very run-down premises in a very run-down inner city, multi-cultural, deprived area. Its past and present tragedies and dramas—and those of our project—are beautifully recorded in our local *Burngreave Messenger*, an outstanding source for local self-understanding.

We said the "Burngreave Ashram" would be "a Christian base in a needy area", and then, a little later "a Sign of the Incarnation, and a Place where Kingdom of God things might happen". What could that all mean in such a situation?

In *The Drama of Mark* (with Morna Hooker, 2010: 51-54), I describe a four-fold "Markan Missional Pattern" whereby Jesus in Mark deals successively with Place—the location of a story, Person—the individual or group presenting themselves, Practice—the practical response of Jesus, and Purpose—the declaration of the significance of the action, often in Realm of God terms.

This sequence was seen in Burngreave Ashram as follows.

1. *Place.* One of the stories of Jesus's first "mission" practice in Mark 2.13-22 relates to his call of Levi and the subsequent meal at Levi's house with a crowd of other tax-collectors, which draws condemnation from the Pharisees. I recall the situation of 80-86 Spital Hill. What could "provide a Christian base in a needy area" possibly mean in this desolate place?

> What had brought us here was the memory of Jesus going among the tax collectors. It had said to us, Find the place nearest to people in   need (51).

2. *Persons.* The Persons? The druggies and the pimps and their ladies on our corner in 2000? We opened the corner shop. We must have a low threshold, we said. But for whom? The people who came in were:

> The typical people of any deprived inner city—people with mental problems or depression, young single mums with their toddlers, failed white middle-class people who could live cheaply in the inner city where their parents would not visit them (52).

Then, we found homeless asylum seekers sleeping on the streets, and let some of them come in and sleep in our cellar (52). Then in 2006 we were able to open residential accommodation where six of them now live, through a co-operative arrangement with ASSIST, the Sheffield Voluntary asylum-seeker support organisation.

3. *Practice.* The Practice was, we learned from Jesus, basically sharing meals. So New Roots for several years financed a Café-Shop, with soup, pasties and home-made cakes at bargain prices. Groups of like-minded people (cf. Mk. 2.15) still come and share meals. The café has become a "community café" and a drop-in for many local people in various need situations, where they find acceptance and at times specific help. A local mental health worker runs a weekly "Knit and Natter" Group.

A weekly commensality of "sitting down with the poor" (John Wesley) is the 6pm Wednesday dinner "Free Meal", recently renamed "Burngreave Banquet", when people on benefits join asylum-seekers and a few homeless people for a lovely hot meal. Those able to do so make a contribution. Much of the food comes from our membership of Fare Share, which delivers unsold food from city supermarkets.

And we have a monthly Sunday lunchtime "Café Church", which attracts an interesting mix of Church also-rans and non-Church seekers. Our theology for these has been supported by John Dominic Crossan's (1991: 66-70) description of Jesus's "Open Commensality". It has helped us along the way, also to Jesus's "Radical Egalitarianism" (Crossan, 71-74). Solidarity and Hospitality belong together.

4. *Purpose.* The Purpose? Our being "A sign of the Incarnation, and a place where Kingdom of God things might happen" means we have a Multi-Faith Chapel and Library, and "welcome those of all faiths and spiritualities, and none." (53-54). In Mark 5, Jesus takes his movement over to pagan territory in Gerasa. In Mark 7 he is inveigled into healing a Gentile woman's child. It makes us reflect much at Burngreave that Jesus' ministry takes him more and more into his multi-faith environment. That's what Kingdom projects are like (55, also Vincent, "Outworkings", 2013).

Our midday all-faiths participatory Seminars, our multi-faith Tree-plantings, our Study Days, our monthly inter-faith Community

Reflections, all follow from this. And a new Mission for Liberation Theology results alongside other faiths.

Reflecting on the Seeds parables of Mark 4 and the tiny Kingdom manifestations there, we comment: "This is the real revolution. This is the famous stone that turneth all to gold! These tiny implantations of seeds are the way the world gets change. So Jesus, according to Mark—and we, following at a distance!" (56)

14. ENDOGENOUS THEOLOGY

Urban Theologising as we have thus described it results in Gospel-coherent, situation-relevant action, action which learns from all the preceding analysis, and is theologically authentic practice. It is practice which is "story-making" (Andrew Davey in Duffield, ed., 1997: 47-52), which story-of-practice then feeds back into theological new creation. Hence, the term "Theological Practice." My article with this title (in *Theology*, 2003) outlines some of the issues. In Andrew Davey's words "through practice, theology has happened" (Davey, ed., 2010: ix).

The concept of "Outworkings" seeks to provide a Gospel methodology for this Practice Interpretation, that precipitates a "Gospel-passage-coherent practice" (Vincent, 2005). Our experience is that there are *methods* whereby "theological practice" can be precipitated. My personal experience is that the Gospel Marks do give one a slant, a predisposition, an expectation, that can be thrown into the Urban Crucible. Our encounters are, on this view, rather more intentional and revelatory than the "blurred encounters" model (Reader & Baker, eds., 2009), though much of what is said under that heading accords with the earlier stages of Theological Outworkings.

So then, Urban Theologising is based upon discipleship, community and political practice, based on the Dynamics of Christ perceived with the help of Gospel models. But now, let us look more closely at what is happening here in the final theological stage, the creation of some new mutations of theology based on the process. Basically, what we experience is new theology arising up out of the theological practice. It is not theology which is "exogenous" (coming from outside), but theology which is "endogenous" (coming from within).

The disciple experiences the significant, either intentionally through theological practice, or unintentionally through reflective discernment. The disciple differentiates what is significant and what is insignificant, and theologises on the basis of certain experiences, realities, happenings and histories. All theology is Contextual Theology in that it is based on living the Christian existence in a particular place, time and culture. All theology is also Endogenous Theology, because it derives from, is created by, and takes its form out of, that which commends itself as significant within the disciple's experience in the context. Endogenous Theologising is the process whereby, faced with the multitude of experiences, realities, happenings and histories, the disciple discerns how what is present represents the same thing as, or can be seen in the same light as, dynamics and trajectories which in the Christian tradition have been and/or are regarded as pieces of theology.

The questions of theologically determined practice, and then endogenous theologising, are developed in *Mark: Gospel of Action*, where contributors describe what they have heard as "calls" in Mark, which lead to settled or experimental practice or discipleship based on the call, and finally lead on to some kind of wider or deeper theologising or globalising on the basis of the gospel inspired discipleship.

The theological practice of Andrew Parker is a life lived on the margins. The endogenous theology concerns the Christological mystery of en-Christedness as being alongside the God of the marginals (Vincent, ed., 2006: 45-52). The theological practice of David Blatherwick is a ministry informed and shaped by Mark's pictures of Jesus and his disciples. The endogenous theology is of a new corporate "son of humanity", of service and alongside-ness in the world (53-61). The theological practice of Mary Cotes is a ministry encouraged and influenced by the women in Mark. The endogenous theology is about Christology, faith and self-discovery among people "on the edge" (79-97). The theological practice of Susan Miller is campaigning for ecological non-exploitation. The endogenous theology is about how "death-dealing forces" are overcome by "a fig-tree whose branches begin to put forth their leaves" (154-163).

In each case, an understanding or realisation of some strand or element or group of stories in Mark's Gospel acts as a provocation and spiritual support for some personal and political practice. The stories, and/or the theology of or in them, or some pieces of story or theology, were experimented with and embodied in a specific person's vocation, activity and way of life. The action is theologically motivated, and thus itself "theological". But then, as that theology-inspired action continues, there arise "signs following", spiritual conclusions, "globalisations". The aspect of discipleship seen initially as a choice based on some element in Mark is then seen as a window of insight into the total mystery of the Gospel, and is brought out as a theological *novum*, or at least a new *mutation*, in a resulting, wider theology which nonetheless still comes from within the discipleship experience—an endogenous theology. The theology-based action, in the course of its operation, gives rise to theological reflection, which issues in the bringing back some new, endogenous, theology, into the theological storehouse of the disciples. The result is an ever-expanding plethora of Urban Mission's "little theologies" (Davey, ed., 2010: xii).

Endogenous Theology could also be a useful label in the area of "ordinary", everyday life. Here, the "Perception of Realities" precedes and precipitates a possible "Naming of Parts". There is no initial intention to be "theological". But if "all things" are discerned anew in Christ, then the "all things" are a possible location for theological discernment. Endogenous Theology thus seeks to follow the "naming" of God-based or Christ-based stories, preferences, practices, but then "secularises" this, and seeks to discern elements of them in secular life. This means a search for, or an awareness or recognition of, elements of existence and politics that within themselves have elements of divinity, along the lines revealed in Christ—the Dynamics of Christ in Politics.

15. LODESTARS AND MANTRAS

You cannot make a "policy" out of Gospel mission experience. But it might be worth recording a few preliminary conclusions I have come to. "Practical Divinity", John Wesley would call it. "Lodestars" I call them— basic strategies or directions which I have come to use, and which I now look out for.

1. *"Where you are is Who you are."* This results from our consciousness of changes achieved by our discipleship of location, and our separation from suburban or academic presumptions to bring "expertises" in from the white highlands. We are a red-lined postcode area, and learn from what that means. Equally, we invite those in suburbia and academia to work out how their locations (environment, finance, employers, colleagues, education, prospects) influence or determine who and what they are, and the interests they represent and interpret other realities and areas in the light of.

2. *"Alongside the Poor."* This is the best we achieve as middle class incarnate practitioners and ministers. And our Academy of UTU likewise is not "for the poor", or "of the poor", but "alongside the poor". You cannot be like the person in need, but you can be "alongside" them, and perhaps even being named as their "friend", as Jesus was by the publicans and sinners, which Jesus was not "one of" but chose to be alongside.

3. *"The Area writes the Agenda: The Gospel writes what you bring to it."* Our slogan insists that the context determines the possibilities and constraints, but that theology determines the practice, which must be both location-specific and gospel-specific. It concentrates not on what you cannot change, but on what you can change, and underlines the need to keep them identifiable and in focus for one's own assumptions and attitudes.

4. *"Practice Interpretation."* We approach the Gospel narratives, dialogues and sayings with two questions. First, what practice resulted from these, or is reflected in these, in Gospel times? And, second, what practice arises today from them? Reception History hopefully also asks these questions of the times between the Gospel and today.

5. *"Theological Practice."* Here we ask the question: What experimental embodiment of a Gospel or Theological Dynamic in terms of Christian activity, community development, group formation or personal witness can we develop which is relevant to the Context that people have? After the Practice, we ask: What are the special or new theological learnings to be brought back from this discipleship or missional practice?

These five "Theo-praxis Principles" when worked out in urban discipleship and mission lead to many different "outworkings", as we have seen in this chapter. They are all *process* and *focus* principles—"lodestars" to look out for and keep your eyes fixed upon.

Beyond them, and living still with a deep hesitation about concluding "policies" from it all, we yet have some "hints" and perhaps "mantras" which we find ourselves concluding and occasionally passing on!

1. Follow your call. Follow your dream. Dig endlessly at the foundational mystery that got you started, or provoked you anew.

2. Go for what is going for you, not for what is not going for you. Don't try to do everything, or you'll do nothing.

3. Have an eye for the main chance (Frank Thewlis). Mission is opportunism for God's Kingdom. You are servicing a movement not running an organisation.

4. Jump on every passing Band Wagon—Government schemes, local co-operators, other churches. But don't trust your project or yourself to them.

5. Always be optimistic. There are always more negatives than positives about everything. Don't pass on negative stories. "Talk up" people and projects.

6. Don't be an answer to people's problems. Create problems for people, with the invitation to participate in God's Kingdom on earth which changes problems into opportunities.

7. When one door shuts, another door closes. It's often initially frustrating, as you could be starting in the wrong place! But don't abandon your vision.

8. Don't bring "services" to "meet the needs" of people. Create a community which out of weakness provides mutual support, so that everyone cares for each other.

9. Create an expectation and a policy which invites and is dependent on people bringing their gifts to the common task. If they think they have no gifts, create openings where they can discover or develop them.

10. Have a low threshold. Make it easy for people to come in. Continue Jesus's "commensality"—sit at table with all who come.

In the next chapter, we move into Politics. We try to see how many of these discipleship practice models, methods and mantras are of use to us as we seek to engage with and speak to the wider worlds of urban community and politics.

Chapter Four

OUTWORKINGS IN

COMMUNITY AND POLITICS

1. DYNAMICS OF CHRIST IN POLITICS

My own commitment to the "Search for Gospel" (New City 6, 1974) in the urban context derived from a conviction that Christianity only made sense if it was "Christocentric", and an equal conviction that the manifestation of that Christ-life had to be "secular-centric", that is, made within practices and projects in secular culture and in the secular world. This I sought to develop in *Secular Christ* (Vincent, 1968), where I argued:

Christ is the way whereby the mundane, the secular, the human, can be given the gift of ultimate significance. ...To believe is to trust that this is really true by being prepared to be lost in actions which will only either work or be justified if, in fact, it is true (166).

"Faith" in the New Testament is thus the preparedness to act in discipleship, community and politics, as if the utterly unproveable—that God accepts what belongs to Christ—were true. It is to "act boldly", as if the hidden were already plain (167). This symbol, this gift, is "both *discriminatory*, restricting itself to the deeds which are found to belong to Christ, and also *indiscriminate*, because all people and all history stand equally before the opportunity of acceptance and entry" (167).

The urban arena, the area of politics, is the place for this Christ-activity, because practice is the origin of it, not spirituality. Christ-practice moves from the outside, the secular, to the inside, the personal, not from the inside to the outside, not from the personal to the secular (167). The secular is the place of his appearing, and the Gospel stories are examples and paradigms of that continual appearing. "What God is Doing in the World" (219-228) are these secular christophanies. Our privilege now is to work with "the Dynamics of Christ" at work in history (201-218).

So that I knew already that the world—the secular—was the place of God's appearing, the place from which the Dynamics of Christ could be working. My first campaigning on Nuclear Disarmament (cf. Vincent, 1962) taught me that unilateral initiative was a necessary part of political action and an appropriate model based on the "unilateral initiative" of Christ. Our 1997 Methodist Report *The Cities* urged Government to adopt "measures to alleviate poverty, tackle racism, restructure the housing market, and remove barriers to employment" (218), and to "invest more resources in children and young people, particularly but not exclusively through high quality education and training programmes" (219). So I was looking out for ways to work politically and locally towards these aims, by unilateral initiative by groups or by governments.

Our Report also opposed competitive bidding (219-220). But in Burngreave, in 2000, we all backed a local bid to be recognised as one of the nation's 39 most deprived areas, to be awarded a New Deal for Communities Grant of around £50 million over a ten year period. In 2001, I was elected to go on its Partnership Board, as a representative for the Voluntary Community and Faith Sector. Now, perhaps, I could see the hopes of *The Cities* Report worked out locally. At the same time, I continued to be involved at the national level, and was present at the Government's Urban Summit of 2002 in Birmingham.

Through all this, how to speak authentically for the urban, and how to speak authentically for the Christian in the midst of and from the urban, were my concerns, and the concerns of the Urban Theology Unit. We were trying to meet Rowan Williams' "challenge" (in Walker, 2005: 22):

How to get theology on to the agenda of planning, locally and nationally (though without necessarily letting on that it is theology).

In this final chapter, I try to get some perspectives from this, in the light of my experiences of the last decade. As that decade has shown welcome involvements of fellow church people, I shall review what has happily now become a growing field of debate—Speaking for the Urban.

But before doing that, we need, as churches and Christians, to face some of the realities which at present influence what people hear us say before we have opened our mouths!

2. SPEAKING FOR THE URBAN

On New Year's Day, 2010, Rowan Williams, the Archbishop of Canterbury, made a moving appeal for people everywhere to open their hearts and think of people in need throughout the world as their brothers and sisters. The Bishop of Sheffield, Steven Croft, made a similar appeal a few days before. Brilliant, I thought.

Then, the next day, a Report is published saying that the 26 Bishops in the House of Lords claimed expenses of more than £1.4 million in a year. The Press cries: Put your own house in order before telling others what to do. (Martin Beckford. 2 January 2010. http://www.telegraph.co.uk/news)

Meantime, Graham and Lowe declare: "If the church spends excessively on Bishops and their houses, there is going to be less in the way of cross-subsidisation and selective allocations to the dioceses, and thus the money demanded from poorer parishes will be greater. It is they who are paying to maintain Auckland Castle for the Bishop of Durham and Rose Castle for the Bishop of Carlisle. It is therefore not difficult to conclude that it is the poor dioceses and parishes that will end up paying for the deficit on the Lambeth Conference" (2009: 134).

The poor parishes continue to suffer neglect:

> The decline in the number of stipendiary clergy is already leading to the closure of a large number of inner city and outer estate churches, with the remaining clergy being asked to take on more than one parish with populations of well over 12,000 (134).

Graham and Lowe say, at present, "financial giving is not underpinned by any sense of mutuality or redistribution between fellow members of the Body of Christ" (135). Outsiders might wonder how a church which thus describes itself can appeal to them to consider redistribution to the poor! Graham and Lowe continue: "There is a very real danger that the Church of England might begin to replicate the growth in inequalities that we are seeing in our nation" (135).

In fact, the poorer urban deaneries pay their way, while suburban ones resent any redistribution as unfair "taxation" (135).

Faithful Cities, though, does not praise or tell the stories of poor churches. Successful town parish churches and cathedrals are praised. Outsiders wonder, however, whether the current revival and success of many cathedrals which are "booming" (Graham & Lowe, 2009: 140), is only possible because they manage to retain finance and prestige and able clergy. There are no surveys of how many poor inner city churches go to the wall so that city centre cathedrals can "sit alongside the other seats of power in their cities" (141).

Certainly, in Methodism, few Central Halls remain. Likewise, little remains in inner cities. Inner city imaginative Methodist projects at Midland Road in Bristol, at Touchstone in Bradford, and Somewhere Else in Liverpool, are based on cashing-in money from former city central missions—which is great for them, but no help almost everywhere else where we have pulled our money out to the suburbs.

Locally, SICEM is now reduced to two ecumenical units without paid clergy (Upper Wincobank Chapel and Burngreave Ashram), plus Pitsmoor Methodist Church, and Shiregreen United Reformed Church.

I fear that all this means that all too often, the churches in inner cities and housing estates are felt to have already "spoken"—by their deeds. Which is, of course, what this book is arguing for, but in an opposite way! Twenty years ago, our erstwhile UTU colleague Austin Smith agonised over it: "One cannot liberate the powerless without radically changing the powerful" (1990: 54). Church policy has yet to catch up. In 2013 Pope Francis's hope for "a poor Church" and a "Christianity of the poor" remains to be fulfilled.

This Chapter is about "Political Practice". We have to start by saying that our practice is political already, in a negative sense. Actions speak louder than words, people say. But some words have led to better action—and could do so again. So, the rest of the Chapter is about attempts to speak positively for the city.

3. AFTER *FAITH IN THE CITY*

Faith in the City (1985) held out the hope that an "alternative theology", a "theology of the city" might be forthcoming. One of the Commission members, Anthony Harvey, wrote of the Commission:

They were asking questions about the nature of 'theology' itself, and suggesting that there may be an 'alternative theology' more appropriate to the needs of Urban Priority Areas (and indeed of Christians in many other places) than the theology which has traditionally been taught in our institutions and which has been regarded as the only legitimate way of giving intellectual expression to the Christian faith. Precisely what forms this 'theology' might take was not a question they sought to answer: it was for 'local theologians' to wrestle with themselves (Harvey, 1989: 1).

Harvey asks, "In what sense can one legitimately speak of 'theologies' in the plural?" He hopes that in the future "the thematic method of this local theology could begin to have a reciprocal and wholesome effect on academic theological education itself" (13).

Due partly to the initiative of former UTU spare-time lecturer Laurie Green, later Bishop of Bradwell, in 1990, Archbishop Robert Runcie set up an Urban Theology Group, related to the Anglican Urban Priority Areas Office. The resulting publication, *God in the City* (Sedgwick, ed., 1995) reprinted two pieces published earlier by UTU, by Margaret Walsh in Wolverhampton (52-71) and Laurie Green in Poplar (72-92).

These "stories" are followed by a variety of contributions intended to give "the sinews of an urban theology". Here, themes of urban life and experience are reflected upon—the Body (Laurie Green), Place (Michael Northcott), Children (Michael Northcott), Black Experience (Novette Thompson), Enterprise (Peter Sedgwick), Crime and Violence (Alistair McFadyen). Three specific aspects of theology are also reflected upon in the urban context—Praise (David Ford and Alistair McFadyen), Sanctuary (Susan Hope) and Transformation (David Ford).

In a final chapter on "Implications", Peter Sedgwick joins significant elements in urban experiences—complexity of relationships, changeability and pluralism, new forms of church life. He concludes: "The Church, like Christ, lives in Galilee, but it confronts Jerusalem … The problem with urban mission is not a matter of will but of imagination" (216).

> These chapters describe, affirm and celebrate the Spirit of God, and ask that such transformation should continue. Equally that transformation will be articulated in new and different theologies of urban life (217).

No attempt is made to develop or to bring together the "sinews" in any wider theology. Indeed, the "sinews" themselves are seen as theological reflections on aspects of urban life, rather than attempts to develop corresponding or consequent elements of theology.

Certainly, the door is closed in the present volume to any claim to create a single Urban Theology. Rather, our volume contains a series of what is best described as "urban theologising"—that is, theological provocation, practice and reflection being undertaken at various points in urban life.

However, it is unfortunate that in the Group's second publication, *Urban Theology: A Reader* (Northcott, ed., 1998), this process is described as drawing on two separate sources:

> The collection of essays with its combination of story, reflection and analysis is designed to chart a new path in urban theology and to exemplify a new way of doing theology in Britain which both draws on the resources of local experience, story and theological reflection in the urban context, and on the skills and disciplines of professional theologians (xi).

But, the two vital elements are separated. First, "the resources of local experience, story and theological reflection in the urban context" are given, but then as an apparently separate contribution, "the skills and disciplines of professional theologians." *God in the City* was mainly written by professional urban practitioners who were skilled in theology, and professional theologians with ministry experience in the urban. But to make the dichotomy exposes the fatal weakness of the plan—to "draw on" two sets of separate material—the local urban material, and the material of 'professional theologians'.

In fact, the *Urban Theology Reader* itself is a full and fascinating collection of pieces from numerous urban theological practitioners, from a variety of sources. But the plan imposed on the different pieces used reveals the weakness of expectation and method. An admirable collection of separate elements of Christian existence and practice in the city is assembled under headings—theology, creativity, shape, sin, poverty, power, generations/gender, work, worship, ministry, mission and faiths. But then, each selection of (uniformly four!) pieces under these headings is prefaced by a scriptural passage, and by a passage from *Faith in the City*. This method indeed illustrates "an intention to link the stories and theologies of urban Christians in contemporary Britain with stories and reflections of urban peoples of God in the Old and New Testaments" (xi).

However, the whole newness of Urban Theology and Urban Theologising is that the scriptural and theological work is done *within* the experience of the urban disciples, and *by* them. It is precisely the experience of urban practitioners that "social analysis and theological reflection on contemporary reality ... turn us back to re-reading the tradition," especially in "the witness of the scriptures" (xii). And also that the witness of the scriptures opens up the social analysis and the theological reflection, we would add.

Three points must be made clear in reply. First, in a true Urban Theology, the practitioners are the theologians. They do not bring in or use outside theological professionals. Second, the contemporary urban experience and the scripture work *dialogically*, from one to the other, beginning at times with experience, and beginning at other times with scripture. Third, the Urban Theology is what results from these two essential elements coming together in dialogue. The Urban Theology is not either of them separately.

4. DIALOGUE WITH SCRIPTURE

We turn to deal in more detail with the relation of scripture to Urban Theology, in this three-fold urban theologising process.

For a start, we would have to admit that dialogue with scripture has had a very marginal place in Church Reports on the city.

The Anglican Report, *Faith in the City* (1985) quotes Paul's "Remember the poor" (Gal. 1.10), and the Good Samaritan, but also observes:

Jesus's proclamation of the Kingdom of God had from the start profound social and political implications. It was to be embedded in a community in which the normal priorities of wealth, power, position and respectability would be overturned (48).

However, "this proclamation took place in the context of an intensely personal concern for individuals, families and local communities" (48). So we are called to work for "a just and compassionate social order" (56), and to community work (57-61). The "Challenge to Theology" is to "attend to the voices, the experience and the spiritual riches of the 'poor' in our midst" (62), to Liberation Theology and "theologies that are authentic expressions of local culture" (65), and to "Theology in Urban Priority Areas" (69).

Faith in the City provided an impetus for many projects through the Church Urban Fund, and for theological work. However, while *Faith in the City* had praised the "shared Bible Study in Base Ecclesial Communities, using scripture to reflect on current social issues in the locality and their experience of community" (80), this was not utilised in the Report's own theological reflection.

We are now, in 2013, in a new situation. The pluralism and multiculturalism of many parts of the Bible is now recognised in scholarly studies and in archaeological work (Rogerson & Vincent, 2009). Likewise, planners and geographers now emphasise the same pluralism and multiculturalism (cf. Sandercock, 2003). A whole new approach to Scripture is opening up, leading to new dialogue opportunities (cf. Baker, 2009: 151-154; Wood & Landry, 2008).

The opportunities for scriptural and theological dialogue in the city are constantly in our consciousness. Crucially, they come at the areas of Christology and Discipleship, as we said in Chapter Two, Sections 13 and 14. Rowan Williams is right when he discerns some of "our scriptures":

Those who now try to be his disciples often have a fair amount of weeping to do over the city; they may find themselves sharing in some measure his exile and rejection from the circles where decisions are made (and so sharing what the deprived and disadvantaged in the modern city know) (2006: 26).

In fact, biblical scholars should be delighted. Their scriptures are being *used*, being *employed*, as spur and solidarity, to change the world! What riches they could take back to the Academy from their scriptures let loose in urban Britain!

5. THE CITIES

In July 1992, a few of us persuaded the Methodist Conference to approve a motion calling for "urgent Action on the Cities", including a call to Parliament to set up a Royal Commission on the Cities, which gained 123 MPs supporting an Early Day Motion request, which was not met.

In 1993, I convened a joint working party of members of the Methodist Division of Home Missions, Inner City Committee and members of Urban Theology Unit, to work at some of the issues. Thirty Ministers and Community Workers met at UTU and outlined problems and issues under ten headings—Exclusion from Society, Growing Poverty, Keeping People in Poverty, Education, Neglect of Community, Racial Issues, Young People, Government Policies, Transport and Housing, and Homelessness.

We put these together in a document, *A Petition of Distress from the Cities*. It was presented at Buckingham Palace and at 10 Downing Street on Wednesday 21 April 1993 by three of us—the 1992–93 President of Conference, Revd (later Baroness) Kathleen Richardson, the Home Mission Secretary, Revd Tony Holden, and myself, who had been President in 1989-90.

In 1994 the Methodist Conference was persuaded to have proposals brought for the Conference of 1995 to set up a Working Group to complete a detailed report, along the lines of *Faith in the City*, ten years earlier. The result was *The Cities: A Methodist Report* (1997), launched in the House of Commons on 5 March 1997.

The Report summarises concerns like those of the *Petition of Distress*, with details from Regional Hearings. It then (205-214), outlines "a theology for today's city" based on scriptural themes of Creation, Incarnation, Cross and Resurrection, and Pilgrimage.

Creation. The city is above all a place where humanity shares in divine creation, even "gaining the upper hand", producing a modern city that has "proved hostile to human flourishing", though its money and power "may foster good" (207). In a common creation shared by all, we need to "work together in pursuit of the common good", even though "commonality seems continually threatened by selfishness". It is in our shared interest to challenge injustices (208).

Incarnation. Christianity celebrates "Jesus come among us all, as one of us, participating in the common life around him, rejoicing that in him all things hold together, and that the created order serves a recognisably human purpose" (209). It sees the need for and the reality of the continuation by contemporary Christians of the ministries of Christ in the city, as incarnate presence, as healer, as parable-teller, as acted parabler, as disciple group creator, as crucified one, as resurrected, and as ultimate fulfilment (210).

Cross and Resurrection. In the city, for many, the pain of unbearable personal suffering felt now "brings the prospect of the cross". By sharing that suffering with one another, we can be blessed with the experience of resurrection. The dead are raised! (211)

Pilgrimage. Cities themselves are on a journey—parts decay, others regenerate (212). Theology is not about simple solutions and grand schemes for change, but about wrestling with insights from inside and outside the church. It is about a pilgrimage through daily life in which Christians seek to respond openly to the whole of human experience. That commitment is to a just and compassionate God, who has revealed in

Christ an equal concern for us all. There is no male or female, Jew nor Greek, slave nor free. God places equal value on the lives of each human being and asks of us that we do the same (214).

This Theology leads to a call that the future city must be more economically prosperous and vital, be more socially just, be safer, be more sustainable, and have a stronger sense of community life (216). The great enemy is social exclusion. "Policies which encourage social inclusion in our cities are not only morally right, but also make sound economic sense" (218).

In general, one would have to observe that the specifically scriptural and theological elements exercise a general influence, but are not used in relation to specific issues.

6. FAITHFULNESS IN THE CITY

More evidence of local Christian Communities using scriptural passages and themes as provocation and support for practice in the city is found in the Report *Faithfulness in the City* (Vincent, ed., 2003). Urban practitioners declare "This is That" (cf. Acts 2.16)—our happening now "is" what a scripture passage describes (216). Three examples will indicate this.

Frankies is a Youth Club and Café in Heartsease Council Estate in Norwich (Peter Howard: 76-85). The question, "What theology can we do with our experience?" leads them to see how they have in fact been led to embody pieces of the Gospel story—good news for the poor (Lk. 4.18), seeing people without a shepherd (Mk. 6.34), creating a sheepfold (Jn. 10.7ff), lifting burdens (Mt. 11.28), sharing feasts (Mt. 22.3ff), using meagre resources (Mk. 6.38ff), being foolish people who confound the wise (I Cor. 1.27), entertaining angels unawares (Heb. 13.2).

Greg Smith reflects on a "Christ of the Barking Road" (100-119), and finds five Gospel "journeys, passages, movements from one place to another, 'roads' along which new revelations appear" (110-115):

The Jericho Road (Lk. 10.25-37): the faithful saved by the foreigner.

The Jerusalem Road (Lk. 19.23): prophetic protest and politics against God and Causes.
The Emmaus Road (Lk. 24.13-35): unknown companions and revelations.
The Road to Africa (Ac. 8.26-30): opening up to us the black disciple.
The Damascus Road (Ac. 9:1-9): conversion to the city.

Geoff Curtiss's account of ministry in Hoboken, New Jersey (120-141) brings together the two decisive themes of this present volume.

First, it describes seven Gospel stories of Jesus which lead to picking up this issue or that, taking certain methods, assumptions and "stands", choosing certain "partners" or "target groups":

"Give them something to eat" (Mk. 6.30)
"When did I see you hungry?" (Mt. 25.31ff)
"Let the children come to me" (Mk. 10.13ff)
"Who are my brothers and sisters?" (Mk. 3.31ff)
"Don't put a lamp under the bushel" (Mk. 4.21ff)
"Go and buy the field" (Mt. 13.44)
"A hundred-fold now" (Mk. 10.29ff)

All these Gospel slogans and vignettes become springboards for actions, mission statements, policy ideas, or suggestions for disciples seeking their way.

The second impetus is the biblical project for justice. Here the key is in classic texts like Psalm 82.1-4, Micah 6.6-8 and Isaiah 58.2-10, plus the tradition of the Jubilee in Leviticus 25.36 and Luke 4.16-20. The Justice tradition led to "Gospel actions" by which this church brought justice to specific oppressed groups.

The conclusion becomes clear from these two threads. The dominant Old Testament theme of justice is pursued in terms of the Gospel Practice of Jesus. In turn, the Gospel Practice of Jesus is the model whereby the biblical concern for justice finds focus and practical outcome. The New Testament records of Jesus and the presence and practice of the Kingdom of God on earth combine both threads. "The street-level Jesus practice is part of God's justice. And God's justice is the final aim of all Gospel street practice" (222).

7. FAITHFUL CITIES

The *Faithful Cities* Report of 2006 revived many questions of concern to Christians in cities. The Report criticises the concerns of "the regeneration industry" to get deprived areas and people economically active.

> Whereas we argue that regeneration should be centred in the people and their well-being, the Government's focus remains largely economic (59).

However, the Report equally urges Christians into "partnership" with local and national government policies for regeneration. Indeed, the Report's "Big Idea" is that of "faithful capital". Following the economic model itself, it argues that group activity and cohesion build "social capital" which helps build up a city. Faith communities, including the Christians, it is argued, bring also a distinctive "faith capital" (2-3).

The idea of "faith capital" has revived the debate as to whether Christians primarily make their witness and do their work in the city as parts of the general "body politic", contributing to "the common good" by common commitments and work, or whether they make their contribution mainly by living out parables and projects of their own distinctive witness—being "in the city" without being wholly "of the city". In other words, is this a time for Romans 13 or for Mark 13?

The idea of "faithful capital" has caused just such questionings. Kenneth Leech (2006b: 15) responds to the Report thus:

> While I am aware that 'capital' in this kind of language—social, spiritual, religious, faithful capital—is being used metaphorically, I think this does run the risk of losing the nature of capital as part of an exploitative relationship between capital and labour. Resources only become 'capital' in the strict sense within this relationship. The literature on social capital seems weak in regard to class, and much of it reflects the current global neo-liberal

agenda with a stress on mutual aid and self-help but not on the reduction of the capitalist class's share in the total social product.

The London Methodist Inner City Group concluded:

The Report seems unable to address directly the economic forces that drive our society. There are occasional references to market capitalism, e.g. how it declines "if the market is populated by people who exercise self-restraint". But there is no indication that there might be any other form of economics than market economics, and no exploration of how the latter, running rampant, damages the common good (Haslam, 2006: 5).

Chris Baker adds a further hesitation based on the experience of churches which try to join in government-led "regeneration":

The rapid re-branding or reorganisation required by faith groups to be eligible for what are often short-term funding pots within an unstable and constantly changing policy field means that they become ideologically separated from their own sources of funding and donor bases, who often seek to preserve original visions and values. These donor bases may be smaller in terms of funding potential, but they are usually more stable and long-term than external sources of funding. In other words, funding is separating faith groups' religious capital from their spiritual capital (Baker, 2007: 22).

Perhaps what we need is not some new participatory scheme which assumes that "we're all in it together, at a common task." Perhaps a real growth in diversity and irreconcilability has to be welcomed. Andrew Davey (2007: 17) speaks positively of "the contested city", and comments:

Faithful Cities is aware of the many claims made on the city but does not take the risk of celebrating the potential creativity of disorder. What do we expect from our urban communities? Do our expectations of a controlled, ordered, settled, harmonious community clash with the reality of ambiguity and contradiction and conflict? How do we use the dialectical tensions and negotiate the real differences we find around us?

A report from Greg Smith of the Centre for Institutional Studies based on surveys in Preston states that all faiths involved in city issues of regeneration and community development have common core values (Smith, 2006):

- Peace and co-operation
- Social justice and equality
- Loving your neighbour

As Smith's report concludes, none of these is the monopoly of the Judeo-Christian tradition. My own experience with inter-faith work and regeneration work in inner city Sheffield bears out this conclusion.

If we now see the key in such generalities, which all faiths naturally support, and which fit in with the general mood of enlightened politicians, what actually does any particular faith contribute? Indeed, does anything remain? It does not have to be distinctive or unique, but there is still the question about what arises authentically from the Christian and especially biblical tradition which might be relevant in the city.

The theology of *Faithful Cities* is reduced to repetitive banality in its use of theology and scripture, as in sentences like: "The idea that, in Christ, God occupies a space in this creation is a mighty affirmation of a doctrine of space (1.22).

But what else could happen on earth except "occupying space"? The point is not "a space", but—as the New Testament constantly specifies—*which* space. God occupies a space at the *bottom* of society. This is an affirmation of a doctrine not of space (newly invented!), but of *specific, disputed* space, *marginal* space, *exploited* space. Or, again:

The story of Pentecost and the origins of the Church encapsulate, in narrative form, an idea of the Spirit as something that harnesses human difference into a coherent version of the Kingdom—a new common dwelling place for humanity in the image of God. That vision of unity amidst diversity is a powerful story for plural and fragmented cities (1.24).

But the plurality and fragmentation are surely not "ironed out" or even "brought together" by Pentecost. Rather, each hears the good news "in their own language" (Acts 1.21). The diversity is legitimised in that the single project of Kingdom is localised in plural character. The New Testament story of Pentecost and early Church is denuded of its distinctiveness if it is forced into supporting the idea of unity amidst diversity. In fact, the New Testament and early Church stories support what clearly existed then—ever-growing diversity amidst a specific, limited unity.

8. REFLECTIONS ON REPORTS

It is perhaps now worth reflecting on the experiences and results of these four Reports—*Faith in the City, The Cities, Faithfulness in the City* and *Faithful Cities.*

I was not personally involved in *Faith in the City,* although our UTU Situation Analysis was quoted in detail (without acknowledgement!) as its Parish Audit (367-372). I was Co-Chair of *The Cities* report, and co-ordinator for *Faithfulness in the City.* The *Faithful Cities* Commission on Urban Life and Faith held a notable day at UTU, and I was part of the CULF Consultation at Church House, though not involved in the Report's compilation.

The *Faith in the City* and *The Cities* Commissions both held extensive Public Hearings in various cities. *Faith in the City* and *Faithfulness in the City* both told significant stories from local churches, especially from ministers. *Faith in the City* and *The Cities* both have extensive chapters on urban realities—poverty, unemployment, work, housing, health, social care, education, law and order, violence. They both also debate specific local and national government policies. They both conclude with Recommendations for Action by Church and by State.

From my experience with *The Cities* and with *Faithful Cities* (at a distance), two problems seem endemic in the writing of Church Reports.

First, the Churches' keenness to involve appropriate professional expertise—planners, sociologists, commentators, politicians—inevitably means that the theologians and church practitioners are drawn into current professional perspectives. Especially, *Faithful Cities* wants to be taken seriously by urbanologists, planners and policy makers, as do the other Reports. This is problematic both because any perspectives are questioned by fellow professionals, and also because it means that only biblical or theological elements get mentioned which seem to fit into or confirm the chosen professional biases. The theology not in *Faithful Cities* had to wait for the later volumes of Graham and Lowe (2009) and Davey (ed., 2010)!

I recall a crucial stage in *The Cities* Working Group. At a Day's Hearing in Newcastle, we had the usual stories of population decline, benefit dependency, homelessness, high crime rates and unemployment, with low school staying-on rates, and few new firms (57). Then, a Report from the CBI outlined their problems. They told how intending industrial entrepreneurs always do a tour of the towns and housing estates near to their proposed sites. In many cases, the areas are so run-down that the entrepreneurs move on and find somewhere else. Suddenly, the local authorities were galvanised into action. The estates had to be cleaned up, or new development would not come. So, from this motivation, the looked-for improvements began to be set in place, in order to impress possible developers. So, we concluded: We were really on the side of economic development, as the only way to deal with urban problem areas. The rest, as they say, is history.

A second problem is that the churches' theologians and practitioners are likely to be "experienced" clergy, who by now are removed from the parish "front line", and are in administrative or leadership posts. Thus the St. Deiniol's Urban Theology Collective perhaps inevitably was the only group of current involved practitioners, and their pastoral and community experiences in *Faithfulness in the City* simply never created the necessary clout, though the ideas were much more in line with the down-to-earth testimonies and realities of *Faith in the City* than the somewhat "ten feet above the ground" *Faithful Cities*. Joe Hasler makes similar points about the voice of the authoritarian Church drowning that of the grass-roots (2006).

Perhaps this is simply one of the results of another regrettable fact—that most ministers of any denomination whom I have known as pioneering and committed inner city, city centre and housing estate practitioners in their thirties and forties are no longer there in their fifties and sixties, but have been picked off by the denominations to fill posts "higher up" the ecclesiastical ladders, as Tutors, Archdeacons, Chairs or Bishops. However much they may regret it, their perspectives change. As we found ourselves saying in UTU and SICEM forty years ago, "Where you are is Who you are".

One special matter which arises from the Churches' Urban Reports is the wider question of whether and how Church and State can or should be in "Partnership"—a question newly posed in 2013 by the debate about the Big Society.

9. PARTNERSHIP

Traditionally, in England, the "Church by law established" has assumed that it would act as the "religious arm" for the city and the state. Now, *Faithful Cities* states that "the Church of England today sees more clearly that its establishment—with the echoes of past power and influence—sits uncomfortably with dwindling memberships" (2.67), at the same time as there are "many other vibrant expressions of religion—including newer Christian expressions and the growth of other faiths" (2.69). All these faiths have "common core values", such as peace and co-operation, social justice and equality, and loving your neighbour, but none of these are "the monopoly of the Judeo-Christian tradition" (7.18).

This means that the Old Testament tradition of religion working together with the state, which had been continued with a state church, now is replaced by a variety of faiths with common values. The distinctive Old Testament values of justice, equality, reconciliation and human rights are therefore now to be represented by a cross-faiths coalition, not a single "Church by law established".

But this forces one to question the cross-faith justice coalition, not just the State Church. Does the New Testament not offer an alternative model? As we have seen, it seems to be concerned with a counter-cultural movement of small peasant or artisan communities on the fringes of great religions and states, living and developing their own separate (they would say, prophetic and kingdom-centred) existences in the nooks and crannies of the great Empire.

One problem for Christians in the city today, faced with the negative effects of their disappearance as Church within the body politic, and their positive position as faith communities alongside other faith communities, is to face the reality that the Old Testament values are now not their peculiar or special gift. And does this mean that the marginal, counter-cultural New Testament model is now more appropriate? (cf. Rogerson & Vincent, 2009: 96-97). Behind that is the wider question as to whether Christianity itself more appropriately functions not as a religion for all, but as a special contribution within faiths of the particular values of the New Testament ethic of indigenous prophetic and counter-cultural living.

The present situation of Church and Nation in Britain makes this a very relevant issue. The New Labour Government declared that it wished for faith communities to co-operate (*Working Together*, 2004). But the evidence of faith representatives who do so is generally that they feel that they make little difference either to the consultation process or to the outcomes (*Faith in LSPs*, 2006: 27-28). Many faith communities have their doubts about participating from their own point of view. "Faith" in urban regeneration has often not worked. Within faith communities, local experience is that "faith" as a form of Social Capital sometimes works and sometimes does not work (Furbey et al, 2006)—be it as bonding, bridging, or linking (7-8; 50-55).

For every proposed Partnership, there are several vital elements that have to be considered. First, who is the proposed Partner? What is their track record? What previous experience of working with this Partner has to be considered? Second, what does this Partner wish to accomplish? What is the end product they demand and work towards? Thirdly, why has this proposed Partner come to us? What part do they see us playing? What of their purposes is fore-grounded by their approaching us—rather than others—as potential partners? Fourthly, how are our distinctive aims furthered?

As Rod Garner says (2006: 137):

As Local Strategic Partnerships impact on marginalised communities, there is a need to ensure that what is perceived by others as practical solutions for specific problems are also to some degree compatible with the distinctive values, concerns and needs of the local church.

Again, should faith groups be in partnership with Government and Local Authority to "deliver services"? It might fit into the theories of sociologists and urbanologists who are concerned to develop "whole cities", "balanced communities", and "participative local democracy". But it also comes at a time when efforts are being made for understandable pragmatic reasons to deal with the perceived threats to society in general originating in the growing multiculturalism of the cities. Two experiences lead me to varying conclusions.

1. My first experience is of nine years helping organise the Manpower Services Commission funded Sheffield Churches Community Programme Agency (1981–88), with 160 workers in 5 centres. We set down the Pros and Cons of Partnership (Vincent, 2000: 61):

Advantages
Projects
   have opened our eyes to society, politics, decision-making, urban needs, people in personal need;
   have produced some worthwhile things—services to people;
   have enabled the churches to open up to the local communities;
   have provided salaries or money to do things which otherwise would not have been done;
   have permitted us to provide worthwhile jobs for individuals for a year;
   have meant that we focus on some specific needs for a time;
   have given some people significant insights and openings into new possibilities;
   have produced salaries for people who want to do a job they wouldn't otherwise be able to do;
   have allowed a few people a way of keeping body and soul together while they perform or discover a personal ministry.

Disadvantages

However, Projects

have made us into business people and employers;

become a pain and burden to us if we are landed with it forever;

mean that employed people from outside do work that ordinary members would do;

have prevented us from being fully alternative, or developing our own self-generated projects;

have meant that ultimately, project-providers, not ourselves, determine what is done;

merely prop up the consumer society in which we are just kept in limbo, and we never tackle the basic issues

2. Then, ten years' experience on the Partnership Board of Burngreave New Deal (2001–2011) leave me feeling deeply ambiguous. We have achieved improvements in terms of education, employment, economic growth, and "additionality" in local government services. However, many of our concerns and campaigns were too easily taken out of our hands, and used to bolster up grandiose schemes. "We need a supermarket" meant for locals just that. It is a call now met by Emin's, next door to Burngreave Ashram. But that was not the interest of the regeneration industry. A mega-Tesco at the bottom of Spital Hill was what we were interpreted as needing. As Schneider and Susser (2003: 4) observe, Urban Regeneration can lead to further "grounding":

A foremost and often over-riding goal is to generate profits for transnational corporate interests associated with finance, name brand shopping, and tourism.

The verdict is still open, in my view. Meantime, I commend James Jones's ten reflections on Local Leadership in New Deal for Communities (2009: 288-289).

10. PUBLIC THEOLOGY

The recent emergence of the notion of "Public Theology" has raised the question as to whether Urban Theology is a Public Theology. In a sense, we might reply, of course, Urban Theology takes place in the public realm, uses as far as possible the language of the public sphere, and speaks about public life. But that would only mean that Urban Theology has always been a "Public Theology". What is added by the term has yet to be demonstrated. So far, it seems to be, like so many new theological labels, a way of becoming more public for some theology of some theologians who do not otherwise have a "public" beyond fellow theologians. But just using the term "Public Theology" has not issued in any "public" interest in or reception of it.

Urban Theology is always totally determined by public issues. But public issues invariably come with Local Problem labels.

Thus, *Faithful Cities* (14) wants to "democratise theology":

So we see theology as the grammar of faithful practice by the disciple which offers a rich repository of stories, rules of life, values and visions by which people can faithfully live their lives under God.

But it is still academy and church and even politics which determine what the "discipline" and the "rich variety" is which is "offered".

We referred in a previous section to Urban Theologising as also theologising about "things going on in the patch". In that sense, Urban Theologising is certainly a Public Theology. But that needs to be said in a way faithful to what we have described. Under the "things going on in their patch", must obviously be included the many movements, developments, plans and programmes of local groups or local authority or national policy. All these are the areas of activity within which and alongside which the local Christian community has to "do its things". Sometimes, these issues and possibilities will loom large in its life and necessitate new arenas for its participation. And properly so. But the Christian community was there before these pressing issues and possibilities, and it will be there after them. So that each of them, when it comes along, will be totally engrossing for some of the Christian community's energies. And the Christian community might re-envision or re-position itself within them. But it will not act as if the issues of deprivation, or gang violence, or social exclusion—much less those of planning, or city strategy, or urban geography, or social policy, or environmental studies, are themselves Urban Theology, or their own prime calling.

In this sense, Urban Theology derives, repeatedly, distinctive and special character precisely from the special areas in which it is encountering particular realities and disciplines. This we have seen in reference to planning and to street culture. These are "Public Issues", and Christians, from their theologies and more particularly their theologising, do something political about them, and also get them spoken about in their local press, radio and TV. They experience an enrichment in their theologies as a result. This is the stage of "bringing back the harvest" into the Christian storehouse (Vincent, ed., 2003: 296-297). An even more significant result is, hopefully, the departure of public issue professionals loaded with a few theologically generated "goodies" which enlarge, enliven and enrich—but possibly expose—their theoretical and practical doctrines.

Indeed, recent "Public Theology" debates have been stimulated not by churches or theologians, but by the Occupy Movements, which have seen a salutary "democratisation" and "horizontalisation" of public issues (Rieger & Kwok, 2012: 40). See the studies by Chris Howson and Noel Irwin in our *For Church and Nation* (Rowland & Vincent, eds., 2013).

Here, we must insist that the *perspective* is important, and the *personnel* are even more important. Urban Theologising is the fruit of actual discipleship, project-making, street-walking, happening, celebrating, spiritual maturing, and revelation-discovering done by disciples and disciple communities. So long as theology is done primarily by academy or church or politics, it is done by those who owe their theological insights not to some restraining and determining secular context or to their vocations in that context, but to the presuppositions, assumptions and rewards of academy or church or politics. It is too often the academy or church or "public" theologians who invent "titles" for what the practitioner-theologians are doing—which is the opposite of what we have discovered and wish to see extended. As in *For Church and Nation,* "Public Theology" is best done from within, by practitioner/theologians actually involved in public life—Community, Politics, Political Action, Protest, Economics, Policy Decisions.

A crucial question which keeps emerging from our study is the question of the *consequential* theology, the *derivative* theology, that comes from theological reflection upon faithful theological practice. *Faithfulness in the City* (2003: 301) concludes from its urban mission stories:

Noticeable is the more or less complete absence of theology as "the great truths" or "the revealed doctrines". If the Sunday liturgy had spoken in any way (as it well might) of a God of power, or of might, or of Lordship, there is little or no indication of it here. Indeed, the classic truths of the Trinity, or of the God of love, or of providence are missing, or at least not articulated. Not surprisingly, it is assumed that there is no point in praying "for those in power", as it is they who are the perceived enemies of the common people. The great churches of the cathedral or the city or the suburbs might assume that they have some natural affinity with the powers, or people in authority, and expect them to be "on the same side", or even that the churches should be their collaborators. But that is not the assumption of the congregations described in this book. And a God made in the image of the powers (whether civil servants, politicians, social workers or ecclesiastics) has no witness here.

Wati Longchar, (2007), hopes for "an Indigenous People's Theology and Spirituality", based on indigenous Asian cultures. Urban Theology has some starters. Hopefully we are seeing the beginnings of Endogenous Theology—theology that rises up within the organism of urban discipleship and mission; theology not from outside (Exogenous) but from within.

11. MORAL, BUT NO COMPASS

This latest Report, *Moral, But No Compass* (2008) was a probably unwelcome broadside exposing government prejudice against churches, and particularly the Church of England. But it also produced more scriptural/theological practice/policy than almost any other. It begins:

When it comes to faith communities in general, and aspects of charity law and social policy in particular, the government is planning blind, and failing parts of civil society (13).

"The Government has good intentions, but is moral without a compass", the Report accuses. It ignores "the Church's huge moral and civic contribution".

Certainly, the government of whatever shape has to do more than give token nods occasionally towards the Third Sector. And the Third Sector has to do much more to involve faith communities at the grass roots level. New structures for "Co-operation" and mutual "Partnership" need to be created at the bottom, involving statutory providers and local congregations. Whether there is the will for this remains to be seen. So far, there is little or no sign of genuine neighbourhood mutual recognition, and no preparedness for policies and projects to "rise up" from local needs or from local possibilities.

However, what might "rise up" is in this latest Report specified in distinctive scriptural/theological insights, "key themes or principles" that might be brought by churches deciding whether and how to involve themselves in "contracting" with the state for the delivery of social or community services (88-91).

1. *Sacrifice and Gift.* Churches "give" themselves to local communities, seeking no "return". So they look for "unconditional moments of gift", which might mean missing a Whitehall "target".

2. *Covenant and Consistency.* Churches are in it "for the long term". So they look not for short-term contracts but for covenants, binding commitments which are long-standing and which build civic capacity consistently and with focus on "implementing long-term visions and being innovative rather than constantly chasing funding".

3. *Voice and Prophecy.* Churches serve "as a 'voice' and advocate for the poorest and most marginalised in society". So they would want services biased towards "those that current systems are failing". Would this be possible?

4. *Solidarity and Empowerment.* The "Christian principle of subsidiarity" means that "initiatives and actions are undertaken at the lowest feasible level rather than the state running and controlling everything".

These are precisely the kind of scriptural/theological perspectives which we must all now seek to bring to the urban table. From the wealth of perspectives in Chapter Two, Urban Theology would have to say that these are only a small start. The "Little Tradition" which T.J. Gorringe observes in the Gospel needs to be the seed. The place of "the margin" and of a "principled marginality" (Garner, 2004: 106-107) has to be present.

The "Little Tradition" needs to find a corporate place in a reconstituted local democracy. As we said in *The Cities* Report (231):

It is important to *make good the current deficit in local democracy*. This could be achieved by: increasing the proportion of local expenditure which is locally determined; restoring to local authorities, some of the responsibilities which have been removed from them during recent years; and considering the benefits of developing more active, local democratic mechanisms, such as citizens' juries, local referenda and neighbourhood councils (Recommendation 6.4).

This all remains to be done.

12. REGENERATION

Two particular issues have been prominent in all the Reports, and they are decisive not simply as points of principle, but even more because of their practical implications at the grass roots level: Regeneration, and Sustainability. We now consider them both separately.

During 2006–2007, I was the Sheffield Lord Mayor's Chaplain to local Councillor Jackie Drayton, and what follows in this and the next section are points which I made at a Town Hall consultation with David Blunkett and civic officers and councillors on 16 March 2007.

The word "regeneration" means "bringing or coming into renewed existence", or "generating again" in the sense of "giving new and more vigorous life", to do again the process of generation, which means "bringing into existence", or "producing". In biology, to regenerate means "to re-grow or to replace lost or injured tissue". In religion, "regeneration" means to be "born again". (All these nuances in the *Concise Oxford Dictionary*).

Thus, a fundamental aspect of "Regeneration" relates to bringing back again a life which was present previously. In urban or planning terms, this means restoring areas or buildings to their previous life.

In fact, what is called "Regeneration" is in urban planning terms more often in reality "Renaissance". Renaissance means a "renewal" similar to that in the 14th–16th Centuries, with reference to art, literature, architecture and design. Consequently, what we are seeing in current Regeneration projects is in fact a "Renaissance" strategy, of bringing in "better" design, architecture, planning and "improvement schemes", based on major outside investment by Government or Local Authority. Naturally, these "consult" the few local people prepared to get involved.

But the idea of "Regeneration" would have to work from the bottom, with seeds growing within neighbourhoods, local people, initiatives and sustainability. This was essentially the idea behind New Deal for Communities. The verdict of how far this has taken place remains to be agreed.

I was one of the 1,500 at the November 2002 Urban Summit in Birmingham, at which "A New Vision of Urban Living" for towns, cities and suburbs was put forward, which "offers a high quality of life and opportunity for all, not just the few." The decisive features (*Our Towns and Cities*, 2000/2003) are: 1. People sharing the future of their community, supported by strong and truly representative local leaders. 2. People living in attractive, well kept towns and cities which use space and buildings well. 3. Good design and planning which makes it practical to live in a more environmentally sustainable way, with less noise, pollution and traffic congestion. 4. Towns and cities able to create and share prosperity, investing to help all their citizens reach their full potential; and 5. Good quality services—health, education, housing, transport, finance, shopping, leisure and protection from crime—that meet the needs of people and businesses wherever they are.

It concludes, "This urban renaissance will benefit everyone, making towns and cities vibrant and successful, and protecting the countryside from development pressure."

From 1999 to 2008 I convened each December at St. Deiniol's Library an "Urban Theology Collective" of inner city and housing estate ministers, with a few professionals and local activists. Out of those years of consultation, point by point, different perspectives have become clear, as we concluded. Point by point, we replied:

1. At present there is great scepticism about local government and local leadership. We need courageous experiments in well-resourced local neighbourhood government. Is there willingness to change at this level? 2. The physical appearance and structure of buildings needs vastly greater investment not in initial design and reconstruction, but in the ongoing, weekly, costly, labour-intensive care and maintenance of them. Will finance be diverted from over-paid, temporary, incoming experts, and spent on under-paid local maintenance workers? Incoming money must *stay* in the areas. 3. Experience shows that desirable environmental improvements in deprived areas can only be made at the cost of inconveniencing suburban and commercial through-traffic. Would politicians support this? Again, maintenance at the grass roots level is also needed. 4. In the economy of the future, shared prosperity, if it were taken seriously, might well be only at the expense of lower standards for the rich. Are we prepared for this? When is Government prepared to offer models for this? 5. Good quality services in all these departments must be organised, administered and delivered within the deprived neighbourhoods themselves, to help build up local self-regard and improve the actual reception of such services at the local level. Are power-holding prestigious professionals willing to move their offices, if not their homes? (*Faithfulness in the City*, 2003: 303-304).

The 2006 Churches' Report, *Faithful Cities* (58), comments that:

There was little doubt that the focus was on material regeneration of urban communities and the criteria used to judge successful regeneration was usually economic and material. What mattered was the level of economic activity and the appearance of the new communities. Status, power and profit appeared to be far more dominant than issues to do with how people lived and the quality of their living environment.

How far New Deal for Communities modified this is yet to be seen.

It is clear that if an "urban renaissance" is to "benefit everyone", it has to begin with changing the reality and the experience of those in the most deprived areas, from the bottom up. There is no "trickle down". Meantime, the "Inclusive Society" eludes us (cf. Blunkett, 2008).

One day, there might be a "trickle up", from the bottom, as new ways of more appropriate living are discovered in the places of present non-success. This is the alternative "vision of urban living" our experiences look towards, building on local people's own successes and strengths, and building up a new "renaissance" from the basis of the present realities, not from some outside dreams.

Hence, Resurrection is a better term than Regeneration. There is resurrection in the place where there has been death. And the "risen" body has all the marks of the previous body, but it lives again.

13. SUSTAINABILITY

The second major issue relates to how we understand "communities". The "Delivering Sustainable Communities" Summit held in Manchester in 2005 defined sustainable communities as:

- Places where people want to live and work, now and in the future;
- Places which meet the diverse needs of existing and future residents, are sensitive to their environment, and contribute to a high quality of life. They are safe and inclusive, well planned, built and run, and offer equality of opportunity and good services for all;
- Places which are diverse, reflecting their local circumstances. There is no standard template to fit them all, but they should be:

Active, inclusive and safe	Well connected
Well run	Thriving
Environmentally sensitive	Well served
Well designed and built	Fair for everyone

(www.odpm.gov.uk/pub/302/summit2005 report back)

This was further developed in the Sustainable Communities Act of 2007. We had a Sheffield Panel for it from Spring 2010. In recession, "Sustainability" has replaced "Regeneration" as the current buzz-word. It could be for the better. Whether it brings "strong and prosperous communities", as the White Paper of 2008 hopes, remains to be seen.

If the Sustainable Communities "places" are to become realities, we all will have to begin with the communities and neighbourhoods themselves, rather than changing Government or Local Authority policies, finance and personnel. Indeed, these must all be based in communities. Several implications follow:

1. The new policy of supporting "Mixed Communities" needs more input from neighbourhoods which have been "mixed", learning their lessons and sustaining their needs.

2. The new emphasis on "Neighbourhood Renewal" needs to discover ways in which local services have been and could be delivered by neighbourhood co-operatives working with Local Authorities.

3. The debate on "Multiculturalism" needs to shift into areas where different cultures do in fact both flourish and co-exist. Resources should be given to aid or provoke such practice.

4. Communities must have their "capacity" built up so that they are equipped and financed to deliver genuinely participatory decision-making and responsibility-sharing, through imaginative innovative neighbourhood government schemes.

5. Regeneration must become a long-term and constantly renewing process of renovation, new build, interior economic development and cultural growth, led and resourced by State and Local Authority funded community neighbourhood structures.

14. THE BIG SOCIETY

Prime Minister David Cameron has added a new element to the debate about future perspectives with his notion of the Big Society.

To some extent, this builds on the ideas of regeneration and sustainability, but seeks ways whereby all the sections of society can play useful and related parts. Alongside Government and Local Authority, the Third Sector of Charities, Social Enterprises, Voluntary and Faith Projects are to be given a greater share.

Andrew Stunnel, the Minister for Faith Affairs in the current Coalition Government has declared that he wants to see Faith-led initiatives from the bottom. As we noted in Sections 9 and 11, there are distinctive slants which Faith Communities have concerning this.

And, of course, to talk of a Faith Sector at all is vastly beyond the present reality of confused and often conflicting individual and locally sustained but very vulnerable undertakings. Such might fulfil the principled project idea of the present book, but would hardly fulfil a national need except as a spur to others. Numerous "Small Societies" is the reality today, and is the scene which, has to be assumed and perhaps argued for, for the future.

David Lammy's plea (2011) is that society as a whole works best as alliances on the ground of communities that have their own strong internal controls and vocations. Lammy says:

Our society needs to reconnect with other important, informal regulators of behaviour—notions of decency towards others, pride, shame, admiration, scorn (53).

In May 2013 the Coalition Government announced "Unlocking Talents" as the key to the Big Society. The previous Government's White Paper *Unlocking the Talent of our Communities* (2008) identifies as key areas: Regeneration and promoting work and enterprise, Encouraging active citizenship and reviving civic society and local democracy, Improving local public services, and Strengthening local accountability. But these were almost identically the aims of New Deal for Communities in 2000.

New thinking is needed. Especially, we do not know how to preserve the "independence" of participating groups (cf. Jones, 2009: 290).

In December 2009, the then Treasury Minister Liam Byrne came with David Blunkett and government officers to a meeting at the New Deal "Sorby House" on Spital Hill in Sheffield to discuss "Regeneration Policies in the next ten years". I suggested we needed to remove "the Regeneration Industry" from its place as arbiters between Government and localities, so that Government dealt directly with community appointed people. The Minister suggested Local Public Service Organisations, which would take local community assets and develop self-help community projects with the local third sector of local community and faith organisations. There's everything to play for, and plenty of experience, even if much is of the "how not to do it" variety. In 2013, the "experts" have disappeared, and fragile local organisations are getting more and more Social Service Provision dumped on them.

The Big Society, of some sort, has been on our UTU agenda for a long time. Studying material for the present volume, I was astonished to find that we had been here before—or was I? In Spring 1974, Francis Butler, Howard Knight and I were in Sheffield Town Hall proposing a "Pitsmoor Project". Our document proposed:

1. That a *Pitsmoor Social Services Project* be set up, for a ten-year period, to replace the existing two sections of areas, with the following specific requirements written in from the outset.

2. That the Social Service Department set up a *Pitsmoor Social Services Advisory Board*, consisting mainly of Pitsmoor representatives, together with representatives from the SSD and the City Council. This Advisory Board would undertake general oversight and responsibility for the township office and for the experimental residential unit, as well as for the project as a whole.

3. That the *general aims of the Advisory Board* be to develop community care, and build up a network of professional and voluntary agencies and persons to exercise care for those at risk and in need.

4. That *multi-disciplinary local facilities* be provided, covering planning, education, social services, etc. The Planning Dept is being asked to set up a local planning office.

5. That the SSD convert an existing property or large shop into a *township SS office*, preferably on Spital Hill.

6. That the SSD set up *an experimental unit* of two to four workers who will reside in Pitsmoor. This would mean accommodation in a house or flat for two to three single workers, plus a family unit.

7. That two or more *community homes* be set up in the Pitsmoor area.

8. That the *Pitsmoor Social Services Advisory Board* be allocated the total amount due for Social Services for its 25,000–30,000 population, and be responsible for developing these and other community based social services provisions for the ten-year period of the project (Vincent, 1982: 56-57).

Is this the kind of thing we need to propose for the Big Society for the future? The present developments seem fraught with problems, as David Isiorho points out (Rowland & Vincent, eds., 2013: 103-112). But Sheffield City Council is turning the New Deal renovated Sorby House into a "Community Hub" for all local Community Services (*Burngreave Messenger,* June 2013). The long-promised "Joined up Thinking" will necessarily mean less output from fewer resources, so perhaps economics is forcing localisation.

EPILOGUE

1. THE FRUITS OF URBAN THEOLOGY

In the Prologue, written in 1973, we held out the hope that the City as a new context for theology might be expected to produce new "messages" from theology. Forty years later, in 2013, we take a contemporary look round at where our "urban theologising" has landed us, taking on board some of the contributions to our recent publication, *For Church and Nation*.

Urban Theology, as we have seen, turns out to be contextual restatements of Christian theology from within the urban, determined by factors of ethnography, ethnicity, sexuality, socio-cultural realities, etc.—which is what one would expect from a contextual theology. Thus, one can certainly not say, "Urban Theology states ...", or "Urban Theology believes ..." Urban Theology is not an agreed set of statements or conclusions, but a constantly reinventing series of theological revelations through the practice of disciples in the city.

However, precisely because of these wide varieties of urban space, identity and politics, Urban Theology is now itself an established "variety" of theology, and that is significant and to be welcomed, provided that it is always seen as a "family" of widely differing urban disciples doing their own "theologising", and coming up with their own distinctive practice and insights.

Thus, Urban Theology has succeeded in achieving a number of things, not least:

1. The recognition that the Urban comprises a legitimate and proper location for theology, alongside the Academy, the Churches and the Theological Seminaries. The presently proposed 2013 Anglican and Methodist Theological Training Arrangements with Durham Degrees needs UTU and UTU-type bases and expectations.

2. An openness to the reception of the actual experiences and practices of urban disciples of differing ethnicities, orientations, cultures, religions and politics, exercising their commitment to aspects of the Way, as they discover them to be possible or relevant within the urban context in its myriad forms as they experience it. See Christine Dutton on "Fresh Expressions" (Rowland & Vincent, eds., 2013: 76-85).

3. A secular-style welcome to specific aspects of life in the contemporary pluralistic city, so that issues, problems, politics, situations and experiences of urban people are received as legitimate material for personal and communal practice and project, leading to theological reflection and theological reconstruction. The genius of Christianity is confirmed as a *secular* mystery. Joerg Rieger and Kwok Pui-Lan thus expound the Gospel tradition of the multitude, the *ochlos,* as key to the Occupy movements (2012: 57-82).

4. A realisation among biblical scholars that the methods of analysis and discernment developed in Contextual and Urban Theologies, in fact are crucial also for biblical studies, and that the practice-motivated approaches of these theologies need to be seen as the kind of "Outworkings" that arose in biblical communities.

5. The harvesting of theological fruit from theologically motivated and liberated action and practice as experimental incarnational witness, ministry, prophecy and community formation, and the potential global and systematic development of such theological fruit in the direction of contemporary restatements of Christianity and Christian truth. The "99%" rather than the present ruling 1% thus achieve a voice. See Noel Irwin in Rowland & Vincent, eds., 2013: 108 and Rieger & Kwok, 2012: 69-71.

6. The recognition of similar and mirroring discernment practice going on in contemporary academic and practical writings in areas of geography, sociology, town planning, and environmental, ethnographic, anthropological and psychological studies; but yet the beginning now of robust critiques from urban theologians precisely within and towards those studies. See Andrew Davey's comments on Planning (Rowland & Vincent, eds., 2013: 132-149).

7. The existence of urban theological resource and research units, not least the Sheffield Urban Theology Unit, with its "long-term commitment to 'urban vocation', through training, incarnational presence and post-graduate research" (*Faithful Cities*: 8.35), and "impressive programme of urban training" (Graham & Lowe, 2009: 144).

8. New Theology/Theologies. How far any distinctive urban theological "goodies" have yet emerged must remain for the future. But *Faithfulness in the City* attempted this, in terms of a fundamental sense of being in line with a genuine essential tradition, confirmed in indigenous experience leading to "endogenous" theological insights:

> The originating dynamic vision in the Old or New Testaments derived from the dreams of the downtrodden, the protests of the persecuted, the mindsets of the martyrs. And, whatever else may be observed concerning our stories, they witness to sudden, unexpected, momentary, but still persistent, gut-level and constantly reinforced identifications of ourselves with the originating characters, locations and commitments of our scriptural and theological forbears. They witness to our *faithfulness*, at the very least, to that tradition (305).

This led to "more grandiose delusions"—"that we have bits and pieces of actuality which can only be described as 'a re-take of primitive Christianity', as 'minimal, essential Christianity', even as 'witness to what God is doing', or 'being part of the thin red line of the apostolic succession of radical discipleship down through the centuries'" (305-306). And then a discomforting reflection:

> Perhaps only when you allow yourself to be put in a situation where there are no other ways to speak about your experience, no other grounds for legitimisation, no other authority for your actions, do human beings in fact resort to, or have need for, biblical tales, or theological insights. We have actions beyond our theologies. We are doing things whose theology is not yet articulated (306).

Such, then, are some of the achievements of Urban Theology. Many today would regard them, or some of them as significant. We may, in all modesty, celebrate them here.

2. THE CHARISM OF URBAN THEOLOGY

So what, at the end, are the special gifts, the unique charisms, the "pearls of great price" so far of "Urban Theologising"?

As we have seen, various characteristics of theological work in the context of the urban suggest that it might be better to speak of "urban theologising" rather than "urban theology". The activity of "doing theology" is best understood as what is going on when urban disciples and urban discipleship communities carry out and reflect upon their Christian practice. Such "what is going on" might include activities like:

- Holding to elements of faith in an environment threatening to it
- Discovering new elements of faith present in urban experiences
- Rejoicing in a realised commonality with New Testament disciples
- Rejecting doctrine or practice found to be offensive or irrelevant
- Developing doctrine and practice found to be convivial and grace-filled
- Building Christian community as constant new forms of *koinonia*
- Developing spirituality from the bottom, from practice
- Experiencing alienation, loneliness, rejection, anomie
- Delighting in counter-cultural secular spiritual richness and diversity
- Developing or joining in popular campaigns to secure liberation or human rights
- Working with our hands in tactile creativity in projects and buildings
- Learning from many faiths and cultures in local community life
- Building up alliances with strange bed-fellows, secular and religious
- Negotiating with political and social power brokers
- Seeing and holding up what seems to be significant in the life of the streets
- Creating political alliances and projects to embody new policies

- Receiving new gifts from other cultures, religions, orientations and lifestyles
- Rejoicing at vestiges of Christ-practice in "non-Christian" people
- Celebrating mystery in common life

In all of these experiences of "Walking with the Word" in contemporary urban contexts, "urban theologising" is the process going on whereby the disciple and the disciple group get together whatever they can to help, inspire, suggest or even mandate what they do or think or say, what they dream up, what they commit themselves to, and what they do or think about the myriad other things going on in their patch or patches. The instinctive "What Would Jesus Do?" (WWJD) achieves urban and sophisticated contemporeneity (cf. Noel Irwin in Rowland & Vincent, eds., 2013: 110-112).

All this continues to be the call and the charism of Urban Theology and Urban Theologising.

It is not a piece of historical theology, a temporary movement being displaced by other theologies with apparently more contemporary names. It is a continuing dynamic and expectant way of standing with the realities of the present and future of our increasingly divided world, as seen in its cities. It is open-ended and inviting.

The prime privilege and charism of Urban Theology and Urban Theologising is to bear witness to the mysteries whereby the common life of human beings on this planet, thrust together in living spaces of close proximity, large numbers and economic interdependence, sharing their existences for survival, imagination, labour and procreation, are consequently shot through with practices, situations, happenings, relationships and histories which betoken, contain and propel the presence in secular realities of ultimate reality, or meaning, or happiness, or significance—what Jesus represented as the Kingdom of God here upon this earth.

In a sense, Urban Theology/Theologising is more like poetry than science. It is Enchantedness, Enchantment (Gorringe, 2002: 257-259). It is an attempt to describe Christianly what Seamus Heaney, in his *Song*, calls "the music of what happens". It is not so much, in John Banville's words, "the song the verse-maker spins inside his own head", but rather "the common world's melody" (Banville, 2008: 8). It is what Heaney, in his Nobel Prize Address of 1995, describes as:

> The power to persuade that vulnerable part of our consciousness of its rightness in spite of the evidence of wrongness all around it, the power to remind us that we are hunters and gatherers of values, that our very solitudes and distresses are creditable, in so far as they, too, are an earnest of our veritable human being (8).

Urban Theology is essentially about the "Perception of Realities". In a striking novel of ordinary people's lives in an inner city Nottingham street, Jon McGregor (2002: 1) describes what he calls "remarkable things"— small, distinct, special happenings that take place to a small selection of residents in the street.

> If you listen, you can hear it.
> The city, it sings.

> It's a wordless song, for the most, but it's a song all the same, and nobody hearing it could doubt what it sings.

> And the song sings the loudest when you pick out each note.

THE URBAN THEOLOGY UNIT

The Urban Theology Unit is committed to mission, practice and theology in the city and on housing estates, and to the resourcing of ministers and lay people for contextual engagement and discipleship that takes academic work seriously.

UTU is a Constituent College of Luther King House, which is an approved partner of the University of Manchester, delivering programmes leading to an award of the University of Manchester.

UTU's Administrative Office, Archives and Annexe Library remain at Abbeyfield Road, in Pitsmoor. UTU's new Teaching Suite and Library is in the centre of Sheffield at Victoria Hall Methodist Church, offering academic courses in theological education and training, in particular MA & MPhil/PhD programmes through Luther King House.

DEGREE COURSES

MASTER OF ARTS IN CONTEXTUAL THEOLOGY

The programme has been devised with various groups of people in mind: school teachers, ministers and clergy in mid-ministry, lay people, community workers and clergy wishing to extend their knowledge and capacity, especially in relation to understanding the Bible and engagement in our contemporary society.

- Interpreting the Bible in our Contemporary Contexts
- Focus on specific Old and New Testament texts (with opportunity for engagement with Hebrew and Aramaic)
- Contemporary Controversies in Biblical Studies
- Jesus through the Eyes of other Faiths
- Research Issues in Urban Theology

MPhil AND PhD RESEARCH WORK

Over thirty years, UTU has developed a collegial and mutually supportive environment for research work. Currently, our students are completing their theses for the University of Birmingham under the supervision of UTU supervisors recognised by the University of Birmingham. From 2013 we are operating in conjunction with Luther King House in the delivery of MPhil and PhD degrees awarded by the University of Manchester through work primarily undertaken in Sheffield.

OTHER COURSES

Short Courses. UTU also offer less formal courses in Personal Theology and Spirituality, Biblical Hebrew, Biblical Aramaic, Urban Theology, and Mark's Gospel. Sabbaticals and courses tailored to particular needs are also provided for.

Summer Institutes. In July, UTU hold a series of Institutes. These provide the opportunity to discuss and contribute to contemporary approaches to biblical studies and theology. Participants can share papers and debate their research ideas. There is a particular emphasis on Social, Political and Cultural interpretations of the Biblical Text and Theology, and on Practice Interpretation.

MEMBERSHIP

The Urban Theology Unit is an independent ecumenical Registered Charity and Company Limited by Guarantee, run by its members through annually elected Trustees. Members receive mailings three times a year which include *UTU News*, AGM papers, financial and other information, and a yearly publication. The UTU Library is open to all members, and books may be borrowed free of charge. Members attend the UTU Summer Institutes at reduced cost, and opt into Working Groups and other activities as they wish.

Urban Theology Unit,
210 Abbeyfield Road,
Sheffield, S4 7AZ.
Tel: 0114 2435342.
e-mail: office@utusheffield.org.uk

BIBLIOGRAPHY

Asterisked Titles are Indexed

For books prior to 2000, see Vincent 2000: 176-180, and prior to 1982, Vincent 1982: 143-146. For a full bibliography of John Vincent's writing prior to 1997, see Duffield, ed., 1997: 83-90

A Petition of Distress from the Cities, 1993. Vincent, John, ed. London: Methodist Home Mission Division / Sheffield: Urban Theology Unit.*

A Tale of Two Cities: The Sheffield Project, 2009. Thomas, Bethan; Pritchard, John; Ballas, Dimitris; Vickers, Dan & Dorling, Danny, eds. Sheffield University Department of Geography.*

Ahern, Geoffrey & Davie, Grace, 1987. *Inner City God: The Nature of Belief in the Inner City.* London: Hodder.

Aldred, Joe; 2005. *Respect: Understanding Caribbean British Theology.* Peterborough: Epworth Press.

Aldred, Joe, Hebden, Sophie & Hebden, Keith, 2008. *Who is my Neighbour? A Church Response to Social Disorder.* ISBN 978-0-955957-0-2.

Amin, Ash; Massey, Doreen & Thrift, Nigel, 2000. *Cities for the many, not the few.* London: Policy Press.

Atherton, John; 2003. *Marginalization.* London: SCM Press.

Atherton, John, Baker, Chris & Reader, John, 2011. *Christianity and the New Social Order: A Manifesto For a Fairer Future.* London: SPCK.

Baker, Chris, 2007. "Addressing the Involvement Deficit" in *Crucible,* January–March: 16-24.

Baker, Christopher, 2009. *The Hybrid Church in the City: Third Space Thinking.* 2nd edn. London: SCM Press / Aldershot: Ashgate, 2007.

Baker, Christopher & Beaumont, Justin, eds., 2011. *Postsecular Cities: Space, Theory and Practice.* London. Continuum.

Ballard, Paul & Pritchard, John, 2006. *Practical Theology in Action: Christian Thinking in the Service of Church and Society.* London: SPCK.

Ballard, Paul, ed., 2008. *The Church at the Centre of the City.* Peterborough: Epworth Press.

Ballard, Paul H. & Husselbee, Lesley, 2008. *Community and Ministry: An Introduction to Community Work in a Christian Context.* London: SPCK.

Banville, John, 2008. Foreword on Seamus Heaney in *Great Poets of the 20th Century.* London: The Guardian / Faber & Faber.

Barton, Mukti, 2005. *Rejection, Resistance and Resurrection.* London: Darton, Longman & Todd.

Beckford, Robert, 1998. *Jesus is Dread.* London: Darton, Longman & Todd.

Beckford, Robert, 2004. *God and the Gangs: An Urban Toolkit.* London: Darton, Longman & Todd.

Bergmann, Sigurd, 2003. *God in Context: A Survey of Contextual Theology.* Aldershot: Ashgate.

Billings, Alan, 2009. *God and Community Cohesion.* London: SPCK.

Blunkett, David, 2008. *The Inclusive Society? Social Mobility in 21st Century Britain.* London: Progress.

Boff, Leonardo & Boff, Clodovis, 1989. *Introducing Liberation Theology.* Tunbridge Wells: Burns & Oates.

Brewin, Kester, 2004. *The Complex Christ: Signs of Emergence in the Urban Church.* London: SPCK

Burngreave New Deal for Communities, 2001–2012: Annual Reports. Sheffield: Burngreave New Deal for Communities.

Cameron, Helen; Richter, Philip; Davies, Douglas & Ward, Frances, eds., 2005. *Studying Local Churches: A Handbook.* London: SCM Press.

Churches in Action, Where Churches are Making a Difference. 2009. London: Church Urban Fund.

The Cities: A Methodist Report. 1997. London: Methodist Church/NCH Action for Children.*

Cox, Harvey E., 1965. *The Secular City: Secularisation and Urbanisation in Theological Perspective.* London: SCM Press.

Communities in Control: Real People, Real Power, 2008. London: Department of Communities and Local Government.

Croft, Steven, 2009. *Jesus' People: What the Church should do next.* London: Church House Publishing.

Crossan, John Dominic, 1991. *Jesus: A Revolutionary Biography.* San Francisco: Harper.

Curtiss, Geoff, 2003, "Ministry in the Gentrifying Cosmopolis", in Vincent, ed., 120-141.

Davey, Andrew, 2001. *Urban Christianity and Global Order.* London: SPCK..

Davey, Andrew, 2007. "*Faithful Cities*: Locating Everyday Faithfulness", in *Contact*, January 2007: 8-20.

Davey, Andrew, 2008. "Better Place: Reforming the Urbanisms of Hope", *International Journal of Public Theology*, 2, 27-46.

Davey, Andrew, ed., 2010, *Crossover City. Resources for Urban Mission and Transformation.* London: Mowbray.

Davis, Mike, 2006. *Planet of Slums.* London / New York: Bantam.

Dinham, Adam; Furbey, Robert & Lowndes, Vivien, 2008. *Faith in the Public Realm: Controversies, Policies and Practices.* London: Policy Press.

Duffield, Ian K., ed., 1997. *Urban Christ: Responses to John Vincent.* Sheffield: Urban Theology Unit.

Duffield, Ian K., 2011. *Contextual Analysis.* Sheffield: Urban Theology Unit.

Duffield, Ian K.; Jones, Christine & Vincent, John, 2000. *Crucibles: Creating Theology at UTU.* Sheffield: Urban Theology Unit.

Dykstra, Laurel & Myers, Ched, eds., 2011. *Liberating Biblical Study. Center and Library for the Bible and Social Justice.* Eugene, OR: Cascade Books.

Eastman, Michael & Latham, Steve, eds., 2004. *Urban Church.* London: SPCK.

Faith in LSPs? Escott, Phillip & Logan, Pat, eds., 2006. London: Churches Together in England.

Faith in the City: A Call for Action by Church and Nation, 1985. London: Church House Publishing.*

Faithful Cities: A Call for Celebration, Vision and Justice, 2006. London: Church House Publishing/Methodist Publishing House.*

Faithfulness in the City, 2003. Vincent, John, ed. Hawarden: Monad Press.*

Farnell, Richard et al, 2003. *'Faith' in Urban Regeneration.* Bristol: Policy Press.

Forrester, Duncan, 2000. *Truthful Action: Explorations in Practical Theology.* Edinburgh: T & T Clark.

Furbey, Robert, et al., 2006. *Faith as Social Capital: Connecting or Dividing?* Joseph Rowntree Foundation / Bristol: Policy Press.

Galloway, Kathy, 2006. "Singing the Lord's Song", in Stratford, ed., 11-24.

Garner, Rod, 2004. *Facing the City: Urban Mission in the 21st Century.* Peterborough: Epworth Press.

Georgi, Dieter, 2005. *The City in the Valley: Biblical Interpretation and Urban Theology.* Atlanta: Society for Biblical Literature

Girardet, Herbert, 2004. *Cities, People, Planet: Liveable Cities for a Sustainable World.* Chichester: Wiley-Academy.

Glasson, Barbara, 2006. *I am Somewhere Else: Gospel Reflections from an Emerging Church.* London: Darton, Longman & Todd.

Gornick, Mark, 2002. *To Live in Peace: Biblical Faith and the Changing Inner City.* Grand Rapids / Cambridge: Eerdmans.

Graham, Elaine; Walton, Heather & Ward, Frances, 2005. *Theological Reflection: Methods.* London: SCM Press.

Graham Elaine; Walton, Heather & Ward, Frances, 2007. *Theological Reflection: Sources.* London: SCM Press.

Graham, Elaine & Lowe, Stephen, 2009. *What Makes a Good City? Public Theology and the Urban Church.* London: Darton, Longman & Todd.

Green, Laurie, 1992. *God in the Inner City.* Sheffield: Urban Theology Unit.

Green, Laurie, 1997. "Gospel from the Underclass", in Rowland & Vincent, eds., 117-125.

Green, Laurie, 1997. "The Jesus of the Inner City", in Ian K. Duffield, ed., 25-33.

Green, Laurie, 2000. *The Impact of the Global: An Urban Theology.* Sheffield: Urban Theology Unit.

Green, Laurie, 2003. *Urban Ministry and the Kingdom of God.* London: SPCK.

Green, Laurie, 2010a. *Let's Do Theology.* 2nd edn. London: Mowbray, [1990].

Green, Laurie, 2010b "God is a Group? The Persistent Presence of the Holy Spirit", in Andrew Davey, ed., 97-103.

Green, Laurie & Baker, Christopher, 2008. *Building Utopia? Seeking the Authentic Church for New Communities.* London: SPCK.

Grinonneau, Jane, 1995. "City Kids as Signs of the Kingdom", in Rowland & Vincent, eds., 12-29.

Grinonneau, Jane, 2000. *City Kids as Agents of the Gospel.* Urban Theology Unit / Sheffield University, MMin Thesis.

Gorringe, Timothy J., 2002. *A Theology of the Built Environment.* Cambridge: Cambridge University Press.

Haslam, David, 2006. Letter in *Church Times*, 11 August,

Hasler, Joe, 2006. *Crying Out for a Polycentric Church*. Bristol: Church in Society.

Harvey, Anthony, ed., 1989. *Theology in the City: A Theological Response to "Faith in the City"*. London: SPCK.

Herring, Debbie, 2005a. *Contextual Theology in Cyberspace*. Urban Theology Unit / Sheffield University, PhD Thesis.

Herring, Debbie, 2005b. "Virtual as Contextual: A Net News Theology", in Højsgaard, M.T. & Warburg, Margit, eds., *Religion and Cyberspace*. London: Routledge, 149-165.

Hooker, Morna D. & Vincent, John J., 2010. *The Drama of Mark*. London: Epworth Press.*

Hooker, Morna & Young, Frances, 2010. *Holiness and Mission: Learning from the Early Church about Mission in the City*. London: SCM Press.

Hope, Anne & Timmel, Sally, 1999. *Training for Transformation*. 4 Vols. Gweru: Mambo Press / Rugby: ITDG. [1984].

Horsley, Richard A., 2008. *Jesus in Context*. Minneapolis: Fortress.

Horsley, Richard A., 2010. *Christian Origins: A People's History of Christianity Vol. 1*. Minneapolis: Fortress.

Howson, Chris, 2011. *A Just Church: 21st Century Liberation Theology in Action*. London: Continuum

Hunter, John, 1995. *A Touch of Class: Issues of Urban Mission*. Sheffield: Evangelical Urban Training Project / Unlock.

Inge, John, 2003. *A Christian Theology of Place*. Aldershot: Ashgate.

Jagassar, Michael N. & Reddie, Anthony G., 2007. *Black Theology in Britain: A Reader*. London: Equinox.

Jenkins, Timothy, ed., 2008. *Religion in English Everyday Life: An Ethnographic Approach*. Oxford: Blackwell.

Jones, Gareth, 1996. "Interview with John Vincent", *Reviews in Religion and Theology*. August 82-88.

Jones, James, 2009. "Towards a Theology of Urban Regeneration", *Journal of Urban Regeneration and Renewal*, 2.3, Jan–Mar: 283-290.

Kim, Sebastian, 2011. *Theology in the Public Sphere: Public Theology as a Catalyst for Open Debate*. London: SCM Press.

Lackenby, Keith S., 1990. *From Old Chapels to New Church*. Urban Theology Unit / Sheffield University, MMin Thesis.

Lammy, David, 2011. *Out of the Ashes: Britain After the Riots*. London: Guardian Books.

Lawrence, Louise, 2009. *The Word in Place: Reading the New Testament in Contemporary Contexts*. London: SPCK

Learning in Context: The Search for Innovative Patterns in Theological Education, 1973. Theological Education Fund of World Council of Churches. Bromley, Kent: New Life Press.

Leech, Kenneth, 2001. *Through Our Long Exile. Contextual Theology and the Urban Experience*. London: Darton, Longman & Todd.

Leech, Kenneth, 2006a. *Doing Theology in Altab Ali Park*. London: Darton, Longman & Todd.

Leech, Kenneth, 2006b. "The Soul and the City": Samuel Ferguson Lecture, Manchester University, 19 October 2006.

Lewin, Hugh, 1987. *A Community of Clowns: Testimonies of People in Urban Rural Mission.* Geneva: WCC Publications.

Living Church in the Global City, 2008. London: Heythrop College / Cuddesdon: Ripon College.

Longchar, Wati, 2007. "Traditions and Cultures of Indigenous People: Continuity of Indigenous People in Asia". www.asiapacificmea.org/statements/indigenouspeople-wati.pdf

Lynch, Gordon, 2007. *The New Spirituality: An Introduction to Progressive Belief in the Twenty First Century.* London: I.B. Taurus.

Mackley, Margaret, ed., 1990. *UTU in the 80s.* Sheffield: Urban Theology Unit.

Marchant, Colin, 2004. "The Story of Urban Mission in the UK", "Key Biblical Themes", in Eastman & Latham, eds.

Massey, Doreen, 2007. *World City.* Bristol: Polity.

Mata, Michael & Vincent, John, 2001. *Urban Mission: Two Viewpoints.* New York: Board of Global Ministries, United Methodist Church.

McGregor, Jon, 2002. *If Nobody Speaks of Remarkable Things.* London: Bloomsbury.

Moral But No Compass: Government, Church and the Future of Welfare. 2008. Davis, Francis; Paulhus, Elizabeth & Bradstock Andrew eds. Chelmsford: Matthew James.*

Morisy, Ann, 2004. *Journeying Out: A New Approach to Christian Mission.* London: Morehouse.

Morisy, Ann & Jeffries, Ann, 2006. "Apt Liturgy: to lift eyes above the horizon", in Stratford, ed., 60-73.

Nixon, David, 2012. *Stories from the Street: A Theology of Homelessness.* Farnham: Ashgate

Northcott, Michael, ed., 1998. *Urban Theology: A Reader.* London: Cassell.

Northcott, Michael, 2003. "The Word in Space", in Vincent, ed., 244-265.

Our Towns and Cities: The Future. Delivering an Urban Renaissance. 2000. London: DETR/ODPM. 5 Vols, 2003.

Pattison, Stephen; Cooling, Margaret & Cooling, Trevor, 2007. *Using the Bible in Christian Ministry: A Workbook.* London: Darton, Longman & Todd.

Petrella, Ivan, 2006. *The Future of Liberation Theology: An Argument and Manifesto.* London: SCM Press.

Petrella, Ivan, 2008. *Beyond Liberation Theology: A Polemic.* London: SCM Press

Power, Anne & Houghton, John, 2007. *Jigsaw Cities: Big Places, Small Spaces.* London: Policy.

Pridmore, John, 2008. *The Inner-City God: The Diary of an East End Parson.* Norwich: Canterbury Press.

Proctor, John, 2002. *Urban God.* London. Bible Reading Fellowship.

Race, Alan, 2001. *Interfaith Encounter: The Twin Tracks of Theology and Dialogue.* London: SCM Press.

Reader, John, 1994. *Local Theology.* London: SPCK.

Reader, John, 2005. *Blurred Encounters: A Reasoned Practice of Faith.* Glamorgan: Aureus

Reader, John & Baker, C.R., eds., 2009. *Entering the New Theological Space: Blurred Encounters of Faith, Politics and Community.* Aldershot: Ashgate.

Reddie, Anthony G., 2008. *Working Against the Grain: Re-Imaging Black Theology in the 21st Century.* London: Equinox.

Riches, John, 2010. *Contextual Bible Study.* London: SPCK

Rieger, Joerg & Kwok Pui-Lan, 2012. *Occupy Religion: Theology of the Multitude.* Lanham, MD: Rowman & Littlefield.

Rogerson, J. W. & Vincent, John, 2009. *The City in Biblical Perspective.* London: Equinox.

Rogerson. J. W., ed., 2013. *Leviticus in Practice.* Blandford Forum: Deo Publishing.

Roth, Wolff-Michael, ed., 2005. *Auto/Biography and Auto/Ethnography: Praxis of Research Method.* Rotterdam: Sense Publishing.

Rowland, Christopher, 1995. "Reflection: The Challenge to Theology", in Rowland & Vincent, eds., 126-131.

Rowland, Christopher, 1997. "The Journey Downwards", in Ian K. Duffield, ed., 35-48.

Rowland, Christopher, ed., 1999. *The Cambridge Companion to Liberation Theology.* Cambridge: Cambridge University Press.

Rowland, Christopher, 2006. "What Have We Here?", in Vincent, ed., 3-8.

Rowland, Christopher & Bennett, Zoe, 2006. "Action is the Life of All: The Bible and Practical Theology", *Contact* 150: *The Bible as Pastor*, 8-15.

Rowland, Chris & Vincent, John, eds., 1995. *Liberation Theology UK.* Sheffield: Urban Theology Unit.

Rowland, Chris & Vincent, John, eds., 1997. *Gospel from the City.* Sheffield: Urban Theology Unit.

Rowland, Chris & Vincent, John, eds., 1999. *Liberation Spirituality.* Sheffield: Urban Theology Unit.

Rowland, Chris & Vincent, John, eds., 2001. *Bible and Practice.* Sheffield: Urban Theology Unit.

Rowland, Chris & Vincent, John, eds., 2013. *British Liberation Theology: For Church and Nation.* Sheffield: Urban Theology Unit.*

Rowland, Christopher & Roberts, Jonathan, 2008. *Bible for Sinners: Interpretation in the Present Time.* London: SPCK.

Sandercock, Leonie, 2003. *Cosmopolis II: Mongrel Cities in the 21st Century.* London & New York: Continuum.

Saunders, Stanley P. & Campbell, Charles, L, 2000. *The Word on the Street: Performing the Scriptures in the Urban Context.* Grand Rapids, MI: Eerdmans.

Schneider, Jan & Susser, Ida, 2003. *Wounded Cities: Destruction and Reconstruction in a Globalised World.* Oxford: Berg.

Schreiter, Robert J., 1985. *Constructing Local Theologies.* Maryknoll, NY: Orbis Books.

Sedgwick, Peter, ed., 1995. *God in the City: Essays and Reflections from the Archbishop of Canterbury's Urban Theology Group.* London: Mowbray.

Segovia, Fernando E. & Talbert, Mary Ann, eds., 1995. *Reading from this Place.* 2 Vols. Minneapolis: Fortress Press.

Selby, Peter, 1997. *Grace and Mortgage.* London: Darton, Longman & Todd.

Shackerley, Paul, 2007. *The Church in the City: Partnership and Hospitality.* Urban Theology Unit / Sheffield University, PhD Thesis.

Shannahan, Chris, 2010. *Voices from the Borderland: Re-Imagining Cross-Cultural Urban Theology in the Twenty First Century.* London: Equinox.

Sheffield Fairness Commission, 2012. *Making Sheffield Fairer.* Sheffield City Council.

Sheldrake, Philip, 2001. *Spaces for the Sacred.* London: SCM Press.

Smith, Austin, 1990. *Journeying with God: Paradigms of Power and Powerless.* London: Sheed & Ward

Smith, David W., 2011. *Seeking a City with Foundations, Theology for an Urban World.* Nottingham: Inter-Varsity Press.

Smith, Greg, 2003. "The Christ of the Barking Road", in Vincent, ed., 100-119.

South Yorkshire in Search of a Soul. 1975. Sheffield: Urban Theology Unit.*

Stewart, Alex, 1998. *The Ethnographer's Method.* Thousand Oaks / London: Sage Publications.

Stratford, Tim, ed., 2006. *Worship: Window on the Urban Church.* London: SPCK.

Stringer, Martin D., 2005. *A Sociological History of Christian Worship.* Cambridge: Cambridge University Press.

Sugirtharajah, R.S., 2002. *Postcolonial Criticism and Biblical Interpretation.* Oxford: University Press.

Swinton, John & Mowat, Hazel, 2006. *Practical Theology and Qualitative Research.* London: SCM Press.

The Urban Theology Unit. New City 1, June 1971. Sheffield: Urban Theology Unit.

Thompson, Judith, with Pattison, Stephen & Thompson, Ross, 2006. *SCM Studyguide to Theological Reflection.* London: SCM Press.

Towns and Cities: Partners in Urban Renaissance, 2002. 5 Vols. London: ODPM.

Transforming Places, Changing Lives. A Framework for Regeneration, 2008. London: Department for Communities and Local Government.

Unlocking the Talent of our Communties. 2008. Empowerment White Paper. London: Department for Communities and Local Government.

Urban Bulletin. 2011. Annual Information Resource on Urban Mission and Ministry. London: Christian Coalition for Urban Mission, 305 Cambridge Heath Road, London E2 9LH.

Van de Weyer, Robert, 2010. *Against Usury.* London: SPCK.

Vincent, John, 1962. *Christ in a Nuclear World.* Manchester: Crux Press.

Vincent, John, 1968. *Secular Christ: A Contemporary Interpretation.* London: Lutterworth Press.*

Vincent, John, 1969. *The Race Race.* London: SCM Press.

Vincent, John, 1975. *Disciple and Lord: The Historical and Theological Significance of Discipleship in the Synoptic Gospels.* Basel University DTheol Thesis, 1960. Sheffield: Academy Press.*

Vincent, John, ed., 1976. *Stirrings: Essays Christian and Radical.* London: Epworth Press.

Vincent, John, ed., 1977. *Doing Theology in the City.* Sheffield: Urban Theology Unit.

Vincent, John, ed., 1979. *Alternative Theological Education.* Sheffield: Urban Theology Unit.

Vincent, John, 1981. *Starting All Over Again: Hints of Jesus in the City.* Geneva: World Council of Churches.

Vincent, John, 1982. *Into the City.* London: Epworth Press.*

Vincent, John, 1983. "Towards an Urban Theology", *New Blackfriars*, January 1983: 4-17.

Vincent, John, 1984. *OK, Let's be Methodists*. London: Epworth Press.

Vincent, John, 1989. *Britain in the 90s*. London: Methodist Publishing House.

Vincent, John, ed.,1998. *Hymns of the City*. 2nd edn. Sheffield: Urban Theology Unit. 1st edn. 1989*

Vincent, John, 1997. "An Urban Hearing for the Gospel", in Rowland & Vincent, eds., 105-116.

Vincent, John, 2000. *Hope from the City*. Peterborough: Epworth Press.*

Vincent, John, 2000: "Regeneration and Community Capacity Building", *Crucible*, Oct–Dec: 234-241.

Vincent, John, 2003. *Journey: Explorations into Discipleship*. Sheffield: Ashram Press. Rev. edn.*

Vincent, John, 2004. *Radical Jesus: The Way of Jesus, Then and Now*. 2nd edn. Sheffield: Ashram Press.*

Vincent, John, 2004a. "Theological Practice", *Theology*, Sept–Oct 2004: 343-350.

Vincent, John, 2005. *Outworkings: Gospel Practice and Interpretation*. Sheffield: Urban Theology Unit.

Vincent, John, ed., 2006. *Mark: Gospel of Action. Personal and Community Responses*. London: SPCK.*

Vincent, John, 2007. *Discipleship. Pocket Radicals 1*. Sheffield: Ashram Press..

Vincent, John, 2009. *A Lifestyle of Sharing*. Sheffield: Ashram Press.

Vincent, John, ed., 2011a. *Stilling the Storm. Practice Interpretation of Mark 4.35-5.1*. Blandford Forum: Deo Publishing.

Vincent, John, ed., 2011b. *Christian Communities*. Sheffield: Ashram Press.

Vincent, John, ed., 2012. *Acts in Practice*. Blandford Forum: Deo Publishing.

Vincent, John J., . "Outworkings" *Expository Times*

2001: "A Gospel Practice Criticism," 113. 1, 16-18
2002: "Gospel Practice Today", 113. 11, 367-371
2005b: "The Practice of Disciples" (Mk.2), 119. 12. 587-588
2006a: "Disciple Practice Today" (Mk.2), 118. 7. 326-330
2008: "Twelve as Christian Community" (Mk.3), 119. 12. 582-588
2011c: "Urban Mission in Mark 4", 122. 11. 541-538
2013: "Multi-Faith Mission in Mark 5", Website. Publication awaited.

Walker, Andrew, ed., 2005. *Spirituality in the City*. London: SPCK.

Walker, Andrew & Kennedy, Aaron, 2011. *Discovering the Spirit in the City*. London: Continuum Books.

Walker, Paul, 1996. *Beyond Politics and Evangelism: Towards Urban Mysticism*. Urban Theology Unit / Sheffield University, MMin Thesis.

Wallis, Ian, 2006. "Mark Among the Soaps", in Vincent, ed., 188-197.

Ward, Graham, 2000. *Cities of God*. London: Routledge.

Ward, Pete, ed., 2012. *Perspectives on Ecclesiology and Ethnography. Grand Rapids*, MI: Eerdmans.

Ware, Stuart R., 2006. *Theology of the Incarcerated: Views from the Underside.* Urban Theology Unit / Sheffield University, PhD Thesis.

West, Gerald, 1993. *Contextual Bible Study: A Resource Manual.* Pietermaritzburg: Cluster Publications.

West, Gerald, 1999. *The Academy of the Poor: Towards a Dialogical Reading of the Bible.* Sheffield: Academic Press.

West, Gerald, 2007. *Reading Otherwise: Socially Engaged Biblical Scholars Reading with Their Local Communities.* Atlanta: Society for Biblical Literature.

West, Gerald & Zengeli, Bongi, 2011a. "Time for Jesus to Wake Up", in Vincent, ed., 97-105.

Wilkinson, Richard & Picket, Kate, 2010. *The Spirit Level: Why Equality is Better For Everyone.* London: Penguin Books.

Williams, Rowan, 2005. "Urbanisation, the Christian Church, and the Human Project", in A. Walker, ed., 15-26.

Wood, Phil & Landry, Charles, 2008. *The Intercultural City: Planning for Diversity Advantage.* London: Earthscan.

Working Together: Co-operation between Government and Faith Communities. 2004. London: Home Office.

KEY BIBLICAL PASSAGES

Mark 1.14-15	Presence of God's Kingdom	55, 57, 58, 59, 74, 98
Mark 1. 16-20	Call of Disciples	55, 58, 59, 74, 81, 99-100, 109
Mark 1. 32-45	Healing Ministry	48, 49, 53, 57, 72, 78
Mark 2. 15-17	Meals with Publicans	58, 74, 80, 81, 90, 97-98, 103, 101, 110
Mark 3.14	Disciple Community	73, 74, 81, 83
Mark 4. 2-8, 26-29	Sower and Seeds	55, 80, 83, 105
Mark 6. 6-13	Disciples' Mission	59, 72, 74, 80, 81, 109-110
Mark 8. 34	Journey Downwards	51, 60-62, 75, 77, 80, 103
Mark 8. 35	Losing/Gaining Life	53-54, 84, 135
Mark 10. 28-31	Disciples' Common Life	59, 60-61, 72, 74, 81, 122
Luke 4. 17-18	Jubilee	55, 58, 77, 91, 121, 122
Luke 6. 20-23	Beatitudes	35, 58, 71
Luke 14. 15-21	Messianic Banquet	55, 58, 98, 104
John 6. 8	Boy with Loaves	83, 85
Matt. 18. 3	Become as Children	32-33, 55, 122
Matt. 25. 31-46	Christ in Needy	64, 86, 122
Acts 2. 16.	"This is That"	32, 49, 50, 52
1 Cor. 11.1	"Be Imitators"	49, 80-81
Phil. 2. 6-11	Journey Downwards	49, 57, 77
Col. 1. 16, 17	"All Things"	47-48, 77

Cf. also Key Gospel Passages in *Hope from the City*, 181-183

INDEX

Imitation of Christ, 32, 49, 53, 60, 62, 71-73, 74, 79, 80-81, 86, 103-105

Incarnation, 33, 53-54, 58, 59, 60, 72, 73, 74, 77, 103-104, 120, 145

Inmundation, 53, 71, 73, 86-87, 94

Inner City, 11, 15-17, 21, 25, 30, 32, 36-37, 39, 75, 85-86, 91-93, 103-104, 127

Inner City Churches, 21, 89, 90-91, 92, 95, 96, 99, 114

Inner City Retreats, 95

Into the City, Vincent, 1982, 8-10, 29, 73, 74-75, 76-77, 142-143

Iona, 81, 93, 95

Jesus

    Actions of, 56-58, 71-73, 100-101, 120

    Community of, 51-53, 59, 73, 74, 78

    Community Worker, 78-79

    Counter-Politician, 51-53, 57, 59, 71, 72, 74

    Crucifixion, 55, 72, 73, 76, 86, 120

    Friend of Publicans and Sinners, 25, 51, 58, 78, 103, 108

    Gospel of, 55-56, 56-58, 58-59

    Healing Ministry, 48, 49, 53, 57, 72, 103, 120

    Journey Downwards, 54, 57, 58, 71, 74, 77, 78

    Model for Disciples, 57, 60-62, 71, 74, 75, 76, 79-80

    Modern Images of, 71-72, 78

    Movement of, 58-59, 69, 94, 103-104

    Project of, 51-53, 53-54, 57, 58-59, 74, 103-105

    Relation to religious powers, 51, 52, 53, 55, 56, 74

    Relation to political powers, 51, 55, 57, 59, 74

    Resurrection, 72, 73, 76, 120, 139

Journey, Vincent, 2003, 8, 44-45

Journey Downwards, Disciples', 60, 62, 64, 77, 103

Jubilee, Levelling, 51, 54, 55, 58, 104, 122

Judaism, 1st Century, 51-52, 54, 59, 86

Justice, 32, 118, 120, 121, 122-123, 128

Kerygma, 47, 88

Kingdom, Realm of God, 32-33, 68, 71, 74, 75, 98-99, 103-105, 109, 118

Koinonia, 47, 87, 147